The Goal
Be Light In The World

William and Susan Dupley

Endorsements

I've known Bill and Sue for more than 20 years. They are two extraordinary people. They have high-pressure jobs and yet lead a low-stress life. They are gifted in speaking, leading worship, writing, entertaining, etc. They have great stage skills. But more important than these, they love God and seek to live by the teachings of Jesus. As their pastor, I get to cheer them on and at times I've spoken correction. They laugh, they cry, they are real people! This book is about being real. Bill and Sue will take you on a journey out of the hard and complicated and into the "I can do this" realm. I love the stories, the insights and the wisdom contained in this book!

STEVE LONG, SENIOR LEADER,
CATCH THE FIRE TORONTO

The Goal *will help you take two-way journaling and the voice of God into your everyday life, as you journal about the key sayings of Jesus.*

DR. MARK VIRKLER, PRESIDENT,
COMMUNION WITH GOD MINISTRIES

My husband and I were completely blown away by Bill's first book, The Secret Place. It brought us in a much deeper relationship with God. This book is a logical sequel of the first one: living with God, what does it look like in our daily lives. It's written in the same clear language, with a lot of examples. The questions at the end of each chapter help you to apply it to your own life.

Since we read the first book, we've met Bill and Sue several times, and were also guests in their house and family. That's why I know that this book is real, they live it: they are kind, loving, serving people attaching high value to family and they do go the extra mile (and yes, I know the Belgian professor in chapter 10).

ILSE CASSIMON-DESAEGER, SENIOR PASTOR,
PIH CHURCH GLORIEPOORT, BELGIUM

My wife Ros and I were working in Toronto in 1995/96 when the Renewal broke out at the airport church. It was huge and thousands of people were touched. Every night was like a conference. Amidst that we found a home group where Bill and Sue Dupley took us in and parented us through this journey of revival. I since have met many famous people in my 15 years with Iris Ministries—not many *compare to Bill and Sue Dupley—who walk the talk and live what they have written in this book.*

Our lives were (and still are) impacted by these humble lovers of Jesus—who know what it means to walk in the garden with Jesus and sit at His feet. They walk in obedience in a real way with real people. They truly seek to hear God's voice and walk in His love daily—whether at work, home, in a huge conference or in their lounge room. They are truly to us heroes of the faith

STEVE AND ROS LAZAR, DIRECTORS,
IRIS MINISTRIES, MOZAMBIQUE

I have known and worked with Sue and Bill for close to twenty years already, witnessing their hearts and gifts for the Lord and seeing them reach out and communicate very well with people of many different ages and backgrounds. They have written The Goal *as another step in leading worship and preaching the Gospel! It is beautifully done, illustrated and explained in fundamental yet creative ways with much detail, ensuring that this book will bring many to understand both the need and the means to set their Goal well and how to go about achieving the Goal properly with the Lord completing our destiny for His kingdom purpose. I am so proud of them and this book. It is time well spent in setting and going for the one true and worthy Goal!*

YOUNG-WHA KANG, FOUNDER,
FOLLOWERS MISSION, TORONTO

Out of all the people I know, Bill is the one whom I most see demonstrating a passion to see the Kingdom of God coming in his workplace. He combines a hunger to hear the voice of God speak with an equal hunger to see the will of God done where he works. He has demonstrated to me that the imaginary "spiritual/secular divide" is a fiction, as our Father in Heaven wants to speak His heart and will into every situation, family, government and country on earth. This book is timely, as Father God wants us to carry His light, His words and His love to every place He causes our feet to tread, and for the result to be a practical outpouring of His love in a way that can impact the very fabric of our society. Each chapter challenges and then leads us to a place of reflection and hopefully action in our own daily lives."

DAVID WUYTS, PASTOR,
THE LIFEHOUSE, COLCHESTER, UK

THE GOAL

Be Light in the World

William and Susan Dupley

Kingdom Heart Publishing

THE GOAL (BE LIGHT IN THE WORLD)
Copyright © 2016, William and Susan Dupley

Illustrator: Heather Sinnott

All Rights Reserved. No part of this publication may be reproduced, stored in a retrieval system or transmitted in any form or by any means—electronic, mechanical, photocopy, recording or any other—except for brief quotations in printed reviews, without the prior permission of the author.

All Scripture quotations, unless otherwise specified, are from the HOLY BIBLE, NEW INTERNATIONAL VERSION ®. Copyright © 1973, 1978, 1984 by International Bible Society. Used by permission of Zondervan Publishing House. All rights reserved. • Scriptures marked KJV are from *The Holy Bible, King James Version.* Copyright © 1977, 1984, Thomas Nelson Inc., Publishers. • Scriptures marked NASB are taken from the *New American Standard Bible*, copyright © The Lockman Foundation 1960, 1962, 1963, 1968, 1971, 1972, 1973. All rights reserved.

ISBN: 978-1-4600-0652-8
LSI Edition: 978-1-4600-0653-5
E-book ISBN: 978-1-4600-0654-2
(E-book available from the Kindle Store, KOBO and the iBooks Store)

Cover photo provided by the National Library of Australia
http://catalogue.nla.gov.au/Record/1531151?

Orbis terrarum typus de integro in plurimis emendatus, auctus, et icunculis illustratus [cartographic material] / Auct. Nicolaus Ioa Visschero

Cataloguing data available from Library and Archives Canada

To order additional copies, visit:
www.essencebookstore.com

For more information, please contact:
William Dupley
the.secret.place@rogers.com
Kingdom Heart Publishing
Carlisle, Ontario

Printed in Belleville, Ontario, Canada by *Essence Publishing.*

Contents

Foreword 9
Acknowledgements 11
Personal Action Plan 13
Introduction 15
Be the Light of the World 19
Love the Lord 33
Love Your Neighbours 43
Family 55
Abide in Me 65
Honour Your Parents 73
Render unto Caesar 79
Go the Extra Mile 85
Stewardship 91
Leadership 103
Seek the Kingdom of God 111
Appendix A: Making Disciples 119
Appendix B: Biblical References of What Jesus Wants Us to Accomplish 123
Appendix C: The Kingdom of God 141
Appendix D: How to Hear the Voice of God 151
Appendix E: How to Be Closer to God 159
Authors Biography: William and Susan Dupley 163
End Notes 165

Foreword

The type of love Jesus both modelled and talked about was sacrificial, unconditional and selfless. Transformational! It's the type of love which benefits both the receiver and the giver. It can transform any relationship and any situation. It is costly to practice yet more fulfilling than any selfish pursuit. It is the best thing you could possibly pray for.

Michael Jackson sang about the "Man in the Mirror." He said, "I'm asking him to change his ways. And no message could have been any clearer: if you want to make the world a better place, take a look at yourself, and then make a change." You could read through this book quite quickly. But I encourage you to allow the Holy Spirit to show you the "Man (or woman) in the mirror." He will show you many ways to love more practically and effectively, and you will find a greater love and joy in your life. You will also become a blessing to those around you, and receive more of His presence and direction in all the areas of your life.

Paul the Apostle said, *"without love I am nothing."* Love is the highest way of living. It will breathe life into us and all our relationships. This book will remind you of many practical ways of doing that. The words of God work! As you step into deeper obedience to His commands, your Father in Heaven will work with you, and you will never be alone. The weight will transfer from your shoulders to His. The adventure will return to your daily life. Life will work.
Let Him begin to make the change.

DAVID WUYTS, PASTOR,
THE LIFEHOUSE, COLCHESTER, UK

Acknowledgements

To the people who helped us know our Heavenly Father and without whose help this book would have never been created.

We are grateful for Rev. Fred Fulford, who invested his time and love to teach us the Word of God. His pastoral care has always been a model to us.

We are thankful for the care and inspiration of Rev. John Arnott, who has taught us about our Heavenly Father's heart and shown us what grace under fire looks like.

We are thankful to Rev. David Wuyts, who helped us create inspiring challenges at the end of each chapter.

We are thankful for our Dad, who showed us what a father does for the family he loves.

We are very grateful to our friend Carol Fellman, who edited every page to ensure it made sense.

We are thankful to Heather Sinnott for sharing her wonderful artistic gifts to bring to life the images of *The Goal*.

Personal Action Plan

This book is designed to help you develop your relationship with the Lord. At the end of each chapter there is a personal journaling exercise. These exercises will require you to write down what you feel God says to you. Since these words are often very personal, we recommend that you record what the Lord says to you in a separate notebook that you can review with a trusted friend. This will help you to begin your personal journey in developing a deeper place of intimacy and communication with the Lord. If you have never heard God's voice or do not always hear from God, I encourage you to read appendix D to learn how to consistently hear God's voice.

We have included examples all through the book of Father to son conversations. These are short letters we felt our Heavenly Father said to us on each topic in the book. We hope that these short examples will be an encouragement to you to develop your own personal journaling experiences with the Lord. If you would like to read more examples of this type of communication with your Heavenly Father, we have written another book called *The Secret Place*[1] that describes this experience in greater detail.

Jesus was always talking with His Father in Heaven. He said, *"I tell you the Son can do nothing by himself; He can do only what He sees his Father doing, because whatever the Father does; the Son does."*[2] This verse clearly shows that there was a close relationship between Jesus and His Father that was based on continuous communication. Jesus would often take time away from His disciples to have these Father-Son conversations. We encourage you to develop the same practice, and regularly draw away to have conversations with your Heavenly Father.

Introduction

Why am I here? What is my purpose? These are questions that men and women struggle with, most of their lives. I heard a man speak once who said there are four stages in a man's life. When he first graduates from school, he is in *survival*. As he becomes proficient in his field of interest, he enjoys *success*. As he gets older, he needs *significance*. Yet, after men have achieved all three of these, they realize the true key to life is *servanthood*. The Lord wants us to skip this process and begin to practice servanthood right away.

Not all people make it through all four phases, and some get stalled at different points; but God wants us to press on to achieve the goal that is set before us. It is clearly a progression. The apostle Paul likens life to a race. He said, *"Let us run with perseverance the race marked out for us."*[3] He stressed that God has a goal for us to achieve, and that we are to *"press on toward the goal to win the prize for which God has called me heavenward in Christ Jesus."*[4]

The question is, "What is that goal?" Some might think it has to do with doing the right things to earn their salvation to get into heaven, but performance is not the ticket to heaven. Salvation does not have anything to do with performance. Salvation has been bought and paid for through Jesus Christ. It is freely given to us through the Love of the Father. I suggest that the goal is best captured by the words of Jesus. He said, *"You are the light of the world."*[5] We are to be a light in a dark world. Jesus tells us how to do that. He taught us many practical methods and ways that illustrated what being the light of the world looks like and how to achieve that goal.

The Goal

Recently a young family man spoke to me and said he was confused. He said, "I believe in God but I am not sure what to teach my children about God."

This appears to have become a common problem. With all the voices calling out to men and women from the media, it is very difficult to know what to believe, how to live, and what to teach your children. God wants us to know what to teach our children, and how we are to live and to interact with His world. He has designed us all with a unique role and purpose in the world. It is His heart that we discover our role and purpose, and fulfill our destiny.

Jesus gave us the key to this journey in the final words He spoke before He ascended to His Father. His last words were actually a statement of His heart for His church. It is called the Great Commission.

> *"Therefore go and make disciples of all nations, baptizing them in the name of the Father and of the Son and of the Holy Spirit, and teaching them to obey everything I have commanded you. And surely I am with you always, to the very end of the age."*[6]

Jesus outlines several things in this verse that He wants us to do.

First He wants us to go and make disciples. A disciple is a learner (a true Christ-follower). The Lord wants us to help others to progressively learn the Word of God to become a mature disciple (literally, "a learner"). It involves training them in the truths of Scripture and the lifestyle required, and sharing your life with them. It requires a personal investment of time and energy.

Second He wants us to baptize them in the name of the Father, and of the Son, and of the Holy Spirit. Baptism is a conscious decision to identify yourself publicly with the sacrifice of Jesus Christ by being baptized in water. It is far more than a simple ceremony; it's a spiritual transaction. When someone is baptized in water, they identify themselves with the death of Christ and their old man (their old life problems, issues and demonic pressures) is buried in the tank. The process of baptism provides a spiritual structure of rights that enables a believer to live the Christian life and forbids the demonic from having rights on them due to previous mistakes and sins.

Thirdly He wants us to teach them to obey everything He commanded. Some believe that Christianity is a set of rules and the word "commanded"[7] here tends to support that idea. The Greek word used

INTRODUCTION

here for "commanded" is focused on the end objective or outcome. One translator said the word "commanded" comes from the verb "to accomplish" and it is much more about what Jesus wants us to accomplish.

Jesus wants us to become the light of the world and to accomplish that every day.

The transformation of the human heart is the goal of Jesus. He wants us to transform our hearts to be like Him, and not to just blindly obey a set of laws or formula. It is best to consider them as outcomes He would like us to accomplish.

It's our heart that this book will help you understand what those outcomes look like in situations you face every day, and to consider how the world would be different if we accomplished these goals. How would our lives be different if our hearts were focused on accomplishing these outcomes?

Many years ago a man named Sidney Sheldon wrote a book called *In His Steps*. In the book, a few members of a church challenge themselves to ask, "What would Jesus do?" before engaging in all of their everyday situations and encounters. It changed their lives and the lives of their town. I challenge you to consider a similar question by asking yourself to consider what Jesus would want you to accomplish when you face a situation in your life and what would it look like if you were the light of the world in that situation.

We have structured this book into categories of life situations and together we will examine what Jesus wants us to accomplish in each category and what it would look like if we did it. We pray this book will be helpful for you to understand what Jesus would like you to accomplish in your lives, so that your joy may be complete; so that you would know what to teach your children, so that you can make disciples; so that you can bring change to your world.

Yours,

WILLIAM AND SUSAN DUPLEY

CHAPTER ONE

Be the Light of the World

Jesus told us a very profound statement in a special message called the "Sermon on the Mount." He said,

> *"You are the light of the world. A town built on a hill cannot be hidden. Neither do people light a lamp and put it under a bowl. Instead they put it on its stand, and it gives light to everyone in the house. In the same way, let your light shine before others, that they may see your good deeds and glorify your Father in heaven."*[8]

Although most know that Jesus is the Light of the world, He says in this message that we are the light of the world. So let's examine what this means.

One definition of the light of the world is to show hope in darkness, hope in despair, and wisdom in ignorance. Lack rules the world right now—lack of light, lack of hope, and lack of wisdom. As a believer we are to look for light, hope, and wisdom. As we do, the Lord will give it and we will be the light for the world.

When a believer looks for light it will be given to them. Light is a metaphor for insight, clarity, directive, purpose, wisdom, and thought leadership. It is given to lead yourself, and others in the way to go; for example, a practical demonstration of insight occurs when you uncover the root cause of problems both physical and spiritual. When you solve a problem at work, you should call on the Lord, ask for light (wisdom), to solve it and He will give it to you. However He doesn't just give it just for you. He gives it to you for all those around you, your customers, your coworkers, your company and your community. Wisdom is to be shared, to give direction to a company, its people, its products, and its customers.

The Goal

Example: Joseph and Pharaoh's Dream

Joseph in the Bible had 12 brothers. He had issues with his brothers who sold Joseph into slavery into Egypt. In Egypt he went through several situations where he was unjustly treated. In one case he was able to interpret the dream for an individual and as a result was recommended to Pharaoh when the Pharaoh had a need for dream interpretation.

> *"When two full years had passed, Pharaoh had a dream: He was standing by the Nile, when out of the river there came up seven cows, sleek and fat, and they grazed among the reeds. After them, seven other cows, ugly and gaunt, came up out of the Nile and stood beside those on the riverbank. And the cows that were ugly and gaunt ate up the seven sleek, fat cows."9*

Causes of Famine

It is rather alarming that the vast majority of famines throughout history have been caused by environmental factors we had (or believed we had) no control over.

The dream that Joseph interprets, only contains the warning of the seven lean years but the dream also gives the key to resolving the problem. You will notice that the seven fat cows and the seven lean cows all come out of the Nile. This is a critical fact and the solution to the problem is to capture the Nile and create a system of irrigation which is able to have a reservoir of water so that they are able to continue to produce crops and have water even during the seven years of famine.

> *"When American engineer Francis Whitehouse was asked to come up with a scheme to irrigate large portions of 19th-century Egypt, his British employers little realized the astounding conclusion with which he would present them! After surveying the Fayum province of Egypt, he discovered the remains of a huge flood control and irrigation project from the ancient past.*
>
> *"He concluded that the most practical method of irrigating the arid Egyptian desert was to reconstruct the system of irrigation that had been so skillfully put in place 3,500 years previously!*
>
> *"This canal, which incredibly still waters a third of Egypt, appears on modern maps of Egypt under its Arabic name, Bahr Yousef, or The Sea of Joseph.*

> "*Whitehouse reported back to his astonished employers that he had confirmed the existence of a vast lake artificially created by the Hebrew patriarch, Joseph, in the time of the Pharaoh Moeris, and that 'the most practical method of irrigating the arid Egyptian desert was to reconstruct the system of irrigation which Joseph had instituted 3,500 years ago'*"![10]

This is a brilliant insight of light. Not only did Joseph provide for Egypt but for all the surrounding areas and for his immediate family. His own family came to Egypt to buy grain because the famine was so widespread. So God provided for the entire country and his immediate family.

I love that God used this whole situation to bring love and light into Joseph's dark past that had been filled with hatred, betrayal, jealousy, and brokenness. Love, forgiveness, and reconciliation with his family were the fruit of the far-reaching light of Joseph's dream interpretation. Joseph's choice to walk and to act in higher ways despite cruel and unfair situations brought healing to his family and hope to nations.

Now there's another thing about this that's amazing! At the time of Pharaoh Moeris, there were many kingdoms in Egypt. Yet because of Joseph's interpretation and wise counsel, he made his Pharaoh extremely wealthy. People would come to buy the grain. When they had no money, they would sell their animals, and when they had no more animals, they would sell themselves. As a result, within seven years, the entire wealth of the region transferred to this Pharaoh and he became the Pharaoh of Egypt. So why is this relevant?

Today we need leadership in our country and in our businesses that they may attract and create wealth for our country and to our businesses, to keep our country prosperous and our people employed. It is critical to see the call to government and to business as a primary calling where we can be light in these spheres of influence. There has never been a time where there has been a greater need for economic insight and creativity in wealth creation than right now.

Kitimat

We also need Spiritual Insight for our country's economic issues. Pastor Art Lucier of Kitimat, BC was concerned about his town's economy. Two out of the three companies that provided the wealth for his town had closed, and their youth had started to leave town for work opportunities. The Lord directed his church's intercessory group to pray for the economy of their town.

An intercessor for Pastor Art discovered that a hundred years ago, their town had lost the right to be a federal port due to the greed of some of their founding fathers. Kitimat is ice free and an ideal deep sea port. Back in the day, these landowners bought up all the land where the railway was to be located, and then planned to charge the railway exorbitant prices for the land needed. As a result the Canadian railway decided to go to Prince Rupert instead, and Kitimat lost not only the railway, but the status of a federal port as well.

When Art was told of this, he and the intercessory team repented of the greed of their founding fathers. One week later, Joe Oliver, the Minister of Natural Resources of Canada, announced that Kitimat would become a federal port. In addition, the town's Aluminum plant decided to invest 5 billion dollars to rebuild their smelting operation. Shell also announced that they planned to build a 40 Billion dollar Liquid Natural Gas facility.

Art and his team received light from God and changed their city like Joseph did. They brought restoration to Kitimat. Nations are in debt, companies are in debt, people are in debt, and the world needs us to be light using the kingdom keys God reveals to unlock our countries problems.

Business

I was once asked by a company to write a white paper called "Why do good companies fail?" It was a detailed research study on characteristics of companies that failed. After I had completed the research, I understood how to recognize failure, but I did not understand why leadership would allow it to happen. I asked the Lord directly this question. I felt He told me the following:

> *Son,*
>
> *Men who are slothful, greedy, and selfish are not good stewards; in fact these behaviours are the opposite of stewardship. Stewardship requires a person to invest their heart, not just their time. A successful entrepreneur puts their whole heart into their endeavor. It consumes them, they constantly think of ways to improve their products, methods, and market penetration. They invest everything to make the venture succeed.*

As a company succeeds, it takes less heart and commitment to continue to run a company and leaders do not commit their hearts to the firm and this is where the problem begins. The lack of passionate commitment leads to indifference or to a poorly-thought-through approach to the work of management. Indifference becomes a cancer that eats through a company and affects most people. This leads to the downfall of the firm.

Leadership must serve with their whole hearts. They cannot be guns for hire. At HP, look at Bill Hewlett and Dave Packard as examples of this kind of stewardship. These leaders were committed to the firm. They poured their hearts into the firm and all drew strength from their examples.

Leadership is the key in all initiatives. Leaders serve. They serve by investing their whole heart, not just their time.

Son, this can be addressed by:

1. *Deciding, "Am I prepared to give my whole heart or just my time?" Every board member, and every leader needs to make this decision.*
2. *They need to ask themselves, "What would I do differently in this firm if this was the most important thing in my life?"*
3. *Priority is the next key to success. Leadership must decide to implement true solutions, not Band-Aid solutions to these issues. Real solutions take heart to develop; they require people to go the extra mile.*
4. *Leaders must be honest with themselves and ask, "Am I prepared to do this? If not, they should step down and let someone else do it who does have the heart. It would be the best thing they can do for themselves and for their company. They should do something they can put their whole heart into."*

Love,
Dad

I used this insight to provide counsel to my customer and to write a blog that was published. A president of an investment firm contacted me and said that after reading the blog[11] he had to really examine his own heart and decided to retire because his heart was no longer in it. As a result he is now the President of an organization which is helping others. He is much happier and is changing the world. This is all from asking the one simple question of "Why do good companies fail?"

The Goal

I work in the computer industry, so I receive wisdom in that business area because I'm called to be light in the world of my company and customers. Light shows clearly where a company should go, and where a product needs to be developed to be ahead of a competitor. This has happened in my life where I have foreseen a service that is required and then became an instigator to cause that service to come into being. Light shines revelation on what can be and shows the steps to bring it into being.

Relationships

In a person's life when you ask for wisdom in relationships you are receiving light. Relationships can be difficult because of different personalities; but, when you call on the Lord for wisdom, or insight into a situation with your wife, or children, He will give it. When you call for wisdom regarding an issue with the neighbour or another family member, He will give it. When you do what He tells you, you are bringing His light. Your actions become a demonstration to others of how to live, how to act and how to be at peace with others. When you do not retaliate, when you turn the other cheek, when you bless and do not curse, you are moving in the opposite direction to the world and you are light.

When you consider others first in the coffee shop or in a lineup, or on a road where you let someone in, you are moving in the opposite action of the world and you are the light of the world. You are demonstrating His words in action.

Light is the opposite of darkness. The world is very dark. The sexual sins of the world are very pervasive. The internet is a playground of pornography for all manner of deviant behaviour. It permeates society at all levels. No longer do men and women need to go to seedy parts of town or crude stores to fulfill their fantasies. It is now delivered to their home via the net.

By not participating in it, by not promoting it, and by not involving yourself in it, you are light. You show others you do not have to participate in this, you can be free from this addiction. Pornography is a type of addiction. It is drawing comfort from something other than wholesome Godly activities. It is a type of demonic persuasion that destroys marriages, and relationships. Jesus tells us it is a sin to even look at a woman with lust in your heart. For if you lust you've already committed adultery[12] and you defile the marriage bed.[13]

By speaking out and saying we don't do this, we are introducing thought contrary to the world's way and we will bring change. By saying I don't do this, and I don't want to, we are light. Men and women will see there is another way. Most know no other way to live (because of the media), and as such, become more and more deviant in their sexual behaviour as their dependency on sexual deviant drama increases. By saying you don't have to do this, and demonstrating it in your own life, you are light.

Being Visible

I have a friend called Jerry that found that sometimes the Lord provides us opportunities to be light in unusual, and unexpected ways. Jerry was a member of the church, and the leader of their men's group, but when he was young he was a drummer in a rock 'n roll band. His band contacted him and said they were planning to do a reunion concert and could he join them. Although Jerry had not played drums for years he agreed, and began to practice. He soon realized that he needed to play in a live situation to really get his skills back to where they were.

Jerry worked in the radio business and contacted a local promoter and asked if he could arrange for him to sit in and play with a few local bands to develop his skills. His friend arranged him to play at a local blues bar with a few local bands. Initially Jerry was really rusty, but the promoter was patient with him, and coached him. I saw him playing at a Blues bar in Florida. He was playing the blues with a local band, and although he did not get pay to play, he found the experience was very helpful.

He had challenged his men's group that they needed to get out of their comfort zone and go to places they would not normally go, if they were to be an impact for the kingdom. He found that the Lord took him up on that challenge, and he was now playing blues in bars in the area.

He found that over time his relationship began to grow with the promoter and others he made contact with. They began to like him, he was funny and they enjoyed being with him. One day his promoter friend said to him, "Jerry, do you believe in God?" Jerry was able to provide many examples of how God had showed himself to him, and helped him over the years. Jerry was the light of the world in that bar. Jerry also found out that when musicians were dying, they often called on people like Jerry because they were the only believers they knew. They had seen the love of God in their lives and when it was all said and done it was the Christian they wanted to be near. Being light in a relationship takes time, but it produces a great harvest.

Jari

Jari is another example of a believer who lets his light shine in unusual places. Jari is a member of Youth with a Mission. He sets up a booth at New Age fairs and offers supernatural services like spiritual readings, dream interpretation, prayer in spiritual languages, and impartation of healing. Unlike the mediums and psychics at the fair, he gives away all of his services for free and of course he is doing it all in the name of Jesus.

The service he provides are simply the gifts of the Holy Spirit, he just doesn't use Christian words. For example when he gives a spiritual reading, he is giving a prophetic word; when he prays a spiritual language, he is speaking in tongues; when he is does dream interpretation, he asks the Lord for the interpretation; and when he does impartation healing, he prays in the name of Jesus.

He is very careful to use the language of the fair and not Christian words. As a result his booth has an amazing reputation for providing the best supernatural services at the fairs. Mediums come to his booth for advice and he provides prophetic words to these people and as result they become very interested in the Jesus that he serves. One of my friends works in this same type of ministry, and does dream interpretation. He told me that after he gives a dream interpretation he introduces them to Jesus who gives the interpretation and the majority give their lives to Christ on the spot.

The Honest Deal

The honest deal is another way you show light. If you steal from someone, you know that it is wrong. Unfortunately many steal (not by physical stealing) but by not being honest. If you are not forthright and do not fully disclose an issue or problem with the buyer, you are robbing the buyer.

Now in any house there are always things that go wrong but if you commit yourself not to hide anything, to repair as best you can, to have full disclosure, then you are light. There are many people who sell homes without disclosing the problems or attempting to repair them. This does not line up with God's way. Light is demonstrated in honest financial transactions when you sell anything. Finances is one of the key areas where light can be demonstrated. When you give back the extra money that a cashier gives you by accident, you are light. When you go back to a store and pay the difference in a product because they charged you the wrong price, your action is often the only light in the cashier's day.

Generosity

When you give to others, to family, to the poor, and to society, you are light. You show others it is better to give than to receive. Now we are not to give so that we are seen by other men. The Lord is very clear that those who give to be seen of men, have received their reward. However if you are generous to others, people notice and people want to be like that. Giving is a key way light is shown in this society. The poor often give even though they are poor and often the wealthy do not. They hold onto their money where rust and moth will destroy, believing that they can somehow take it with them, but they cannot. Jesus tells us, "Do not store up your riches on earth where rust and moth can destroy, but store up riches in heaven."[14] This is done by giving to others.

I know a woman who has a real knack for this. I have learned generosity from her. She is continually making things like dollies or blankets which she willingly gives away to others. The material costs are small but the time costs are high. When she gives of her time, she is light. She has eyes for the needy. Her gifts speak great volumes to others not just physically, but value is imparted to them by her generosity. She communicates that someone cares, someone noticed and, it breaks despair. When we give to others, it also inspires others to be generous.

Light is shone in every act of kindness you do for another. A kind word spoken, time given to the poor or to an old person is the greatest gift you can give. It is light, which gives hope, and it communicates value and worth. To the beggar on the street who feels so downcast, it communicates value. I remember Peter of Peter Paul and Mary singing a song about the poor. I was always impacted by one line. It said:

> *I'm the cripple on the corner, You pass me on the street*
> *I wouldn't be out here beggin', If I had enough to eat*
> *And don't think that I don't notice, That our eyes never meet.*[15]

This is such a profound statement. Although many give to the poor on the street, very few give them eye contact. It is eye contact that communicates value. The poor do not want pity, they want to be validated, they want hope, and they want life. When we simply look into the eyes of a beggar on the street and bless them and for a moment let your eyes contact their eyes, you shine light, you communicate value and acceptance of them as a human being.

Giving time is the greatest gift you can give. You are truly giving of yourself when you teach another how to a repair a car, or clothing, when you show someone how to use their computer or move their house, or help them plant gardens, or help them build anything. When you share from your life, this is being light.

The righteous in spirit are those who are generous with their knowledge and their heart. Don't hold onto your knowledge, your wisdom and your skills. Give them away. In this way you are demonstrating light.

Showing Kindness

Kindness is the first differentiator. When we are looking out for our own interests, we are not kind, but are self-centred. By simply being kind, attending to a person's physical needs, like bringing them a drink or a coffee, we are being kind. By not being demanding, but being sensitive to others' issues, problems, and frustrations, by being patient and waiting for a person to finish what they are doing, and by not demanding attention, we are being kind. Not being a bully or raging until we get attention is one of the best ways to show kindness.

Consider the person on a helpline, or a cashier who is bullied by a customer all day. Inside they want to scream and lash out at the bully but can't, because they will lose their jobs. They just have to take it. Being kind to them will speak life, and hope into their lives. Consider the gas station attendant who is harassed by a lineup of customers. He needs a kind word, and a word of thanks.

A friend of mine often speaks to bathroom attendants and thanks them for doing such a good job in cleaning up the bathrooms. He told me an incident at the exhibition in Toronto where there was a young heavyset man, who was cleaning the bathroom in the food building at the Canadian National Exhibition. It really was a disgusting job and my friend could see by this young man's face that he was very downtrodden. He simply said, "You are doing a great job, thank you very much for cleaning this bathroom." The young man's face lit up and shone. He asked him if he was going to school. The young man said, yes, that he was in university. My friend blessed his school year and future and that young man felt much better because someone had noticed, someone had cared, someone had been kind and had valued him.

The simplest word of kindness speaks great life to others. God wants His children to focus on the world not the church. We reach the world by our actions not just words. A simple word of encouragement can change a life.

Pray for the Sick

Jesus continually demonstrated the He is the Light of the world by the many ways He healed people. He healed the blind, the lame, and the leper, cast out demons and restored the downcast.

Jesus healed all manner of illness, but not all His healings were physical; for example, when He set free the demonic of the Gadarenes, He restored a man's mind that had been tormented by demonic spirits. When He spoke to the woman at the well, He restored a woman who had been rejected by her neighbours, and He restored her value.

There are many types of healings; some are dramatic like when Jesus raised Lazarus from the dead, or made the deaf hear. Some take some time, like the man Jesus prayed for who was blind; after prayer he told Jesus that he saw men as trees walking. This means that even though Jesus had prayed for him, he still did not see clearly, so Jesus prayed again and then he could see clearly. A simple word given with God's insight, can bring peace and restore a broken heart. Jesus forgave the woman caught in adultery by simply saying, "I do not condemn you, go and sin no more." He released her from her shame.

I have prayed for thousands in the lines at the Catch the Fire Church in Toronto during the revival. I have often received a word from the Lord that encourages me to just say to the person, "You are forgiven." This is healing the sick as much as restoring a broken body.

Example: Man with the Shattered Knee

Praying for the sick is not always convenient. One time Sue was preaching and there was a man in the front row who was wearing a brace on his leg. He had crushed his knee in an industrial accident and was unable to walk without a cane. He had limited motion in his leg and could not fully bend or straighten it. The Lord spoke to Sue and said, "Pray for him." Initially Sue said, "Sure, Lord, after I finish teaching this." She then heard God tell her to "Go and pray for him" (right away) and she stopped teaching, went to the man, prayed for his leg, and then went back to her teaching. A little later in the service she noticed that he was crying. She asked him if she had hurt him. He said, "No, I can't see the scars from my knee surgery." He was completely healed. He took off his brace and did not need his cane. He went back to Edmonton and played baseball with his kids for the first time in his life.

Example: "Ann"

Another time Sue was working in an extended care facility. She was teaching Personal Support workers, and there was a client with dementia we will call "Ann." She had been separated from the other residents because she yelled all the time.

Sue was about to show her students how to approach "Ann" when the Lord said, "Sing Jesus Loves Me, to her." Susan's students were not necessarily Christians; some were Muslim and Hindu, yet she said to herself, "I either hear from God or I don't." She chose to follow the Lord's leading and began to sing "Jesus Loves Me" to "Ann." To her amazement, "Ann" stopped yelling, sweetly folded her hands, and began to sing with Sue. Sue reached down and pulled "Ann" out of her wheelchair and they all walked down the hall supporting "Ann" singing "Jesus Loves Me." "Ann" had sat in her wheelchair and had not spoken for years. Later that day, Sue could not find her students. She found them in the bathroom singing "Jesus Loves Me" as they were showering "Ann." This usually fearful and combative lady was peaceful and calm as the students worked with her. A first!!

The next day the head of nursing came by and Sue said to her, "Do want to see something amazing?" "Ann" was yelling down the hall again. Sue approached her and began to sing "Jesus Loves Me" to her. Immediately "Ann" folded her hands and sang along with Sue. The head of nursing began to cry and exclaimed, "That is amazing." When asked, the family provided a CD player with Hymns. "Ann" knew them all. Even though she was nonverbal, she could sing. The staff began to play the music 24/7. "Ann" became peaceful and calm, and was successfully reintegrated into the client community. At night other Dementia clients would come and stand in the doorway of her room and listen, and sense God's Presence as it filled her room. Years later, a young nurse who had been one of Sue's students, phoned Sue and told her that she was reading scripture to "Ann" late at night after her work was done. She very excitedly reported that "Ann" had spoken for the first time in years. She said, "Thank you for being so kind. I want to go home now." An area of "Ann's" mind had been restored.

Personal Journaling Exercise

1. Think of 3 situations or relationships in your life where you could demonstrate more kindness. Bring these situations to your Father in heaven in prayer, asking for forgiveness and grace as necessary.

2. Thank Him that you are the Light of the World: listen and write down anything He puts on your heart about light.

CHAPTER TWO

Love the Lord

One day Jesus was asked what the greatest commandment was.

"He answered, 'Love the Lord your God with all your heart and with all your soul and with all your strength and with all your mind'; and, 'Love your neighbour as yourself.'"[16]

This is an intriguing statement. How do we actually love the Lord our God with all our heart, with all our soul, and with all our strength and with all our mind? It is clearly an all-encompassing statement.

We're encouraged to love the Lord our God with four distinct attributes of our being, our heart, our soul, our mind and our strength. Each of attributes has a unique capability. Our heart is the centre of our being, having the capacity for moral preference. It is the centre of all physical and spiritual life. In the Bible, we are encouraged to lay a thing up in our heart, to fix our heart on something. That means to plan or purpose to do something. Ideas are conceived in our heart. It is out of our heart that our mouth speaks. Everything we do and say starts in our heart. If the heart is fixed on evil, we will do evil. If our heart is fixed on good, we will do good. I believe it's in our heart where we receive intuition from God. In contrast, our soul is the seat of our feelings, and desires. It is what we feel. Our mind is our intellect. It is our faculty of understanding. It's the way we think. It's our thoughts. Strength is our ability, might and power. It includes our talents and abilities. We are encouraged to love the Lord our God with all these aspects of our being.

The Goal

Heart

Worship is often considered to be the way we love God. In fact we are encouraged to worship. Worship is a complex concept that expresses itself through all four attributes of our being but it starts in our heart. The Bible states that *"out of our heart our mouth speaks."*[17] We are encouraged to *"Worship the Lord with gladness; come before Him with joyful songs."*[18] Worship is demonstrated by our strengths, and we use our mind and the passion of our heart to think up different ways to creatively express our love for God. Lifting our hearts to God and offering, ourselves, our service, our actions, our gifts, and talents, music, art, songs, words, our bodies in movement and in dance before Him, are all acts of worship.

Worship is one way of loving God. Worship is a type of romance. When we worship we speak words of adoration and intimacy to our Heavenly Father. Now ask yourself, do you think that God has to hear that He is great and wonderful? Does He have a big ego and has to be told constantly how big He is? Of course this doesn't make any sense. He is secure, He knows who He is, and He does not need to be told. So He has a bigger reason. I suggest He wants our heart to know that God is bigger than any situation we are facing. When we worship we remind ourselves that God is bigger. Worship is for our benefit. As we worship, the eyes of our heart focus on the *"author and perfector of our faith"*[19] and an impartation of hope, peace, and an awareness of the greatness of God overwhelms us. His presence encompasses us, and our heart is changed.

The Lord encourages us to worship. He says that He is spirit and if we are to worship Him, we must worship Him in spirit and in truth, not just singing songs or doing some type of physical activity like raising our hands or kneeling. Worship is much greater than this. It is loving the Lord our God in everything we do. It is a demonstration of a changed life, in how we behave, how we think, and the things we value.

We attended a funeral of a friend from the Followers Mission in Toronto. He had a very hard life and had a lot of addiction problems but had risen above them. Unfortunately in the process, he contracted AIDS, and after 18 years of the Lord's intervention, he finally died. Yet his life was a demonstration of worship. Over and over individuals came forward and said how he had impacted their lives, how generous he was, how he smiled, and how he was a completely changed man. Every act of his day was an act of worship. He showed he loved the Lord his God by the way he interacted with others. He demonstrated the values his Heavenly Father loves.

Consider this question. How do you show someone you love them? Here are a few ideas a group of our friends had:

- They feel love when people do the things they like for them, sometimes these things are done unseen.

- When others do not do the things that would upset them or make them sad.

- When they are served with an honest heart, with a lover's heart, not out of duty but out of love.

- We show someone we love them by doing things that they like, even though they don't see it.

- We show our family we love them when we clean up the house, wash the toilets, cut the grass, and pay the bills, or other household chores. Actions speak louder than words when it comes to love.

- We show love when we forgive others and do not hold grudges.

If we do the things that our Father in Heaven values, it shows that we love Him. We believe this is true worship.

Soul

Another way we love God is by being thankful and recognizing that He is involved in our lives. God wants us to develop a heart of thanksgiving not just to Him but for everyone and everything. This is the realm of the soul.

How many of you have worked and done things and never had anyone say thank you? Everybody has. Most of us just go ahead and keep doing the work; but when someone says "Thank you," it does something. It changes our heart, and it helps us feel appreciated,

The Goal

Thanking others is a critical component that we need to practice. Not just for the other person's sake but for our sake. When we develop a thankful heart, we do not develop a bitter heart.

- A thankful heart sees the best.
- Is continually grateful.
- Rejoices in life.
- Experiences joy that is complete.

In contrast

- A bitter heart sees the worst.
- Continually complains.
- Does not see the good things in life.

We need to thank God. Let me give you a few ideas of things for which we thank God.

- We thank God we live in Canada. It is one of the greatest countries in the world; many people in the world want to live here.
- We thank God we have healthcare.
- We thank God we have good water, sewage, police systems, good roads, consistent electricity, and safety. Most of the world does not have this.
- We thank God we have food to eat, and a place to live, and we're not cold in the winter.
- We thank God we have a family, and we have a good relationship with our children.
- We thank God for our grandchildren.
- We thank God for our spouses.
- We thank God we can worship freely and openly.
- We thank God we have jobs.
- We thank God we are healthy.

This approach to life changes your heart. It focuses on the positive, not the negative. That is why the Lord says to come before Him with thanksgiving and enter into His courts with praise. If we do these things, it shows that we love Him. This is true worship.

Mind

The word for *mind* here includes your thoughts, your understanding, and your reasoning ability. It can be an instrument of self-destruction when exercised without God's light and power. God expects us to use our mind to reason through ways and techniques to accomplish the things that He has given us to do. This is in contrast to a set of rules which we would follow as if we were robots; for example, the Lord doesn't say specifically how we are to love our neighbour. He expects us to use our mind to do that. He is much more focused on the outcome of our neighbour being loved, than the actual technique that we used to execute that. We love the Lord our God when we use our mind to creatively reason through methods and ideas to accomplish the things He wants done. This is true worship.

We also demonstrate our love for God by what we think about. What occupies our mind? One writer said the battle is for the mind. The apostle Paul supports this statement when He states:

> *"Do not conform to the pattern of this world, but be transformed by the renewing of your mind. Then you will be able to test and approve what God's will is—His good, pleasing and perfect will."*[20]

The process of renewing our mind takes great effort. The majority of us focus a great deal of our mental capability on negative things. These negative things do not help us, nor do they help us to be transformed. The apostle Paul further explains what we should think about. He states:

> *"Finally, brothers and sisters, whatever is true, whatever is noble, whatever is right, whatever is pure, whatever is lovely, whatever is admirable—if anything is excellent or praiseworthy—think about such things."*[21]

He outlined seven categories of thoughts in one verse. Here is a short summary contrasting what we should think about, and what we should not think about.

The Goal

THINK ON	DO NOT THINK ON
True	deception, lies, inaccuracies, phony, insincere, false
Noble	the undignified, the unsophisticated, unrefined, dishonest
Right	what is evil, fraudulent, unrighteous, corrupt
Pure	fake, counterfeit, dark, unholy
Lovely	unhappy, uncaring, repulsive
Excellent	inferior, crude stories, gossip, bad report, poor quality

Thinking on the things that Paul mentions, teaches us how not to conform to the things of this world, and it will actually heal our heart and give us great peace. Thinking and ruminating on negative thoughts, leads to destruction.

I suggest that thinking includes not just what we meditate on with our cognitive capability but what we listen to, what we watch, and what we read. I recently was reading a history novel. It was a very interesting book, though every now and then there were sex scenes in in the book, and I found myself thinking about those scenes after I stopped reading it. As a result, I stopped reading the book because I did not want my mind captivated by these thoughts. This is loving the Lord your God with your mind. It is taking thoughts captive and choosing not to think about those things.

We must constantly be monitoring what our mind is thinking about, what our ears are listening to, and what our eyes are watching. One time there was a television show on that we weren't really watching because we were checking our emails, but we glimpsed a scene that was disturbing. We immediately turned it off because we didn't want to watch what we were seeing. We need to constantly be aware of all that we are exposing ourselves to.

Strength

Each of us has unique strengths and talents and abilities. We are to love the Lord our God with each of our own strengths. I like to preach and teach. It's a strength, and when I use this, I'm loving the Lord my God. Susan loves to play the piano. When she teaches a neighbour how to play the piano, she is loving the Lord our God. My daughter is an artist who hears from God. When she paints she actually is loving the Lord our God. When she teaches others how to hear God and to live out of flow from the Spirit of God, she is loving the Lord our God. The people who cook at the Followers Mission, demonstrate their love for the Lord by their ability to cook for the homeless.

Loving God is personal. We once discussed with others how they love God. Their answers were very diversified and reinforced the fact that each expressed love to God in ways that were unique to their character. Some of the ways we heard were:

- When I appreciate nature.
- When I intentionally worship without being provoked.
- When I intentionally choose to spend time with Him.
- By honouring my body and stepping outside once a day and going for a walk, I break free from the condemnation of work and the tyranny of the urgent and spend time with Him.
- When I have a transparent relationship with God and share the good, happy and sad things with Him.

I asked the Lord what He would say to me about loving the Lord your God. This is what I felt He said to me.

Son

You demonstrate your love to Me when you value the things I love. When you call on Me for wisdom and clarity. When you recognize you cannot do it all on your own, and need My strength to accomplish what I've called you to do. When you sing to Me as if no one else is in the room. When you hold close

The Goal

My concerns about My world, and bring them before Me. These are all evidence that you love the Lord your God.
Love,
Dad

We believe listening to our Lord and doing what He says is loving God. If we do not listen to His exhortations, we're not really loving Him.

Personal Journaling Exercise

1. Think of a time when someone loved you with action as well as just words. Give thanks for that and pray for that person.

2. Look at the key relationships in your life. How could your love and respect be expressed in practical ways? Plan to put these into practice.

3. Think about the phrase "Heart, Mind, Soul and Strength." Ask the Father to activate all those areas in your life. Write down anything He says to you.

4. Develop a thankfulness journal that you write in daily, it will help you foster a thankful heart attitude.

CHAPTER THREE

Love Your Neighbours

"Love your neighbour as yourself."[22]

I was on a plane flying home from Edmonton. It was a full plane and I had worked for many hours and I just wanted to get home. I was exhausted.

My seat was beside a Sikh teenage girl. She had a middle seat and I had the aisle. She asked if I would change seats with her so she could sit across from her Dad.

Initially I said no. I really didn't want to sit in a middle seat for four hours. Then I was reminded of the message I was going to preach on Sunday, on loving your neighbour as yourself so I traded seats with her. The Lord follows His exhortation of loving the Lord your God, with the statement, *"Love your neighbour as yourself."*

"Love the Lord your God with all your heart and with all your soul and with all your mind and with all your strength. The second is this: 'Love your neighbour as yourself.' There is no commandment greater than these."[23]

The heart that loves God will love others because the heart who loves God loves others like God loves them. He gave Himself for them so that He may have relationship with them, not out of duty but out of love.

So we have to ask ourselves, "Who is our neighbour?" Let's just start with our spouse and children. A husband and wife must love each other. They need to serve one another and put their spouse first. This does not mean they are slaves or servants to be walked on, where one is dominant and the other is subservient. It is not a relationship born out

The Goal

of duty. It is a relationship out of intimacy that is so fine tuned to each other's needs, that they meet their spouse's needs without being asked.

The Lord promises to give us the desires of our heart because He loves us, not because we are doing things for Him. He wants to bless us. The key indicator of a heart that is changed is wanting to love others—our wife, children, family, kids, neighbours, and mankind—as ourselves.

Jesus' disciples were once arguing about who was the greatest amongst them. The Lord knowing what they were talking about, said this:

"Anyone who wants to be first must be the very last, and the servant of all."[24]

In another version of the gospel, He made this statement regarding the same situation:

"Whoever wants to become great among you must be your servant, and whoever wants to be first must be slave of all. For even the Son of Man did not come to be served, but to serve, and to give His life as a ransom for many."[25]

Jesus knew what all successful men know, that if you want to be truly great, you have to be a servant of all. Andrew Carnegie learned this late in his life. He was the richest man in the United States in the 1890s. He made his wealth building businesses in the steel industry in Pittsburgh. When he retired, he dedicated his life to giving away his money. He built 2,200 libraries in North America, Carnegie Hall, and many other institutions. As a result, he learned true greatness as a servant. Bill Gates is doing the same thing right now in this generation. He is giving away his money with the specific goal of serving the world. He too has learned that to be truly great, you must become the servant of all.

Servant Heart

I asked the Lord what it means to be servant of all. I felt He said this:

"'I want' is the basic cry of the child. It is self-oriented. It is driven by personal self-satisfaction. It is not concerned with the needs of others. They want their demands met first, regardless of how inconvenient it is, or how self-serving it is. This is the way many people are. They are children. The apostle Paul tells you to grow up and stop being a child and become an adult. He says

to put away childish things and embrace adult things. Adults consider others. They do not think of themselves before others. They are responsible and learn to serve. Many people still have the child reigning in their heart. Although they are older, they are still children who demand and scream to get what they want. You cannot love your neighbour as yourself if all you care about is yourself. This is a true indicator of a child."

The decision facing all of us is whether we will choose to grow up or continue to be children. At the end of this chapter, I will give you an opportunity to decide if you want to address the heart issues that I have been talking about in this chapter. The Lord wants to speak to the child within you and help that child grow up into the adult He wants you to be.

I have known many people who have demonstrated what it means to love their neighbour. Let me tell you about a few.

Mike

My neighbour Mike is really the salt of the earth. He is a teacher and his family has a very busy life. Recently my wife and I went away on holidays in the winter and while we were away, we had a very heavy season of snow. Mike came to my house and shoveled our driveway. He cleared away snow from the furnace and ensured that my house was safe. He demonstrated the wonderful heart of a person who loves his neighbour.

Shoveling snow is such a simple activity yet it gave us great peace to know that someone was looking after our home while we're away.

I grew up with a neighbour named Carl who had the same servant heart. He regularly took care of my parents' home when we were away. This kind of neighbourly care is a wonderful example of loving our neighbours.

The Goal

Steve and Ros

Stephen was a teacher in Australia who came to Canada for a job swap. He was a man full of life who heard from God. He and his wife went to Mozambique after working in Canada and worked for Iris ministries. They run the orphanage in Maputo. As a teacher, he used his skills to develop the next generation in Mozambique as well as take care of the orphans and care for the babies with AIDS. He has a tremendous heart for children and people and makes life fun for them, pouring God's extravagant love and surprises on the poorest of the poor.

Young Wha Kang and Followers Mission

Young Wha Kang was a mother who lived in a very wealthy part of Toronto. She had a heart for the city. She's Korean and could not speak English very well. She was not sure what she could do to bring the kingdom to the city. She looked at what her skills were and decided that she and her sons could give out coffee and sandwiches at the corner of Queen and Sherbourne in the city of Toronto. At that time that area of Toronto was considered the crack capital of Canada, the worst part of the city. Yet she would go down with her kids and just give away food and tell people about Jesus. She has now established a mission in the city of Toronto called the Followers Mission. It has been more influential in leading people to Christ than any ministry I know of in the city of Toronto.

Katrin

Katrin was a young university student who caught His heart for the poor in Africa. Instead of staying in her comfortable home in Germany, she reached out to the poorest of the poor in the garbage dumps of Maputo. Not yet 25 years old, she worked directly with the poorest of the country. Pastoring the dump, she coordinated distribution for food, caring of children, and arranging wonderful little events to meet the physical and spiritual needs of the people who live around the perimeter of the garbage dump. It's dangerous yet none of it seems to bother her. She gave of herself and trusted God in her pursuit of loving her neighbours.

Susan

My wife, Susan, has continually shown me what loving your neighbour looks like. I remember when we were working in a dump in Mozambique with Katrin and a little boy had lost his shoe. The environment in the dump was very hazardous and the loss of a shoe was a serious issue; however, finding a little shoe when there were people everywhere and pandemonium was the norm seemed like an impossible task. Susan picked up the boy, raised his shoe above the crowd and yelled, "Sapato! Sapato!" (which means shoe in Portuguese). Amazingly, someone brought the shoe to her and she carefully put it on his foot. Keeping our eyes open to the needs of others and making efforts towards helping others is loving your neighbours.

The Goal

Sue is continually making things for others. She always has some blanket underway that she's making, or she is knitting something for some young mother somewhere. She always believes that the best way to bring the kingdom is by using whatever you have in your hand, whatever your talents and abilities are. One of the things she has in her hand is her ability to play the piano. She has used it by giving free lessons to small children that show an interest in music.

Loving your neighbour starts with small things. Here are some additional examples that anyone can do:

- Acknowledging a person in the line with you when you're getting a cup coffee, and letting them go first.
- Never pushing ahead.
- Letting people in, in traffic when you are driving.
- Respecting others.
- Giving up your seat on the bus.
- Taking the middle seat on the plane.
- Listening to others, your family, or spouse when you don't have the energy.

Turning the Other Cheek

Jesus told us a very difficult thing to do when we are confronted by difficult people. He said this in the Beatitudes.

> "You have heard that it was said, 'an eye for an eye, and a tooth for a tooth.' But I say to you, do not resist an evil person; but whoever slaps you on your right cheek, turn the other to him also. If anyone wants to sue you and take your shirt, let him have your coat also."[26]

LOVE YOUR NEIGHBOURS

Jesus was not a doormat. He did not let people walk over Him and He doesn't expect us to be one either yet He makes this very profound statement. I don't believe that this verse means that we are not to protect ourselves, or if our country is called to war that we should be a pacifist. There are great evils in the world that often require us to stand up and say, "No farther." Both my Mother and Father served in the Second World War and I am grateful that they stood up and were counted to stop the evil that was trying to take over the world at the time. However, this particular exhortation from the Lord needs to be addressed. How do we turn the other cheek and in what situations do we do this?

I was staying in a hotel with my wife on a holiday once and our neighbours were very loud and drunk and I was getting angry. I called the front desk and they addressed the matter and eventually the people quieted down. When I went to bed, I had an imaginary conversation with these neighbours. I was challenged by the Scripture, *"Love your enemies and turn the other cheek, pray for those who spitefully use you and say all manner of evil about you."*27 I realized this was very difficult and I wanted vengeance. I wanted to scream and yell and tell these loud rednecks to shut up. I judged their heritage. I felt they were ignorant. They had been with us all week, taking up the patio with their whole family, and although I had blessed them even though they were loud, after three days of it, I was fed up and wanted to write a scathing review of this resort and hurt their reputation for not dealing with these yahoos. Then I remembered. *"Love your enemies."*

I thought of the Palestinians who had lost their families and homes due to Israeli rockets. I thought of the atrocities of the Russian Ukraine war, and the abuse of the German soldiers during World War II. I thought, "How does someone forgive this? How do you love your enemies when all you want is justice and vengeance?" I realized this was very difficult. I thought that if I felt confused, and so indignant over some loud drunk people, how does a Palestinian feel? I asked the Lord about these feelings. This is what I felt He said.

Son,
Of all the things I have told people, love your enemies was the most controversial for the very reasons you stated. Man wants vengeance. They want revenge when injustice occurs. That is why movies and books have exploited this theme for years. It is

The Goal

a fundamental desire for man to see the unjust punished, to get their reward. It cries out to the heart of man, to look at all the unjust situations that have occurred in their lives. They draw enjoyment from seeing the evil perpetrators get justice.

The challenge with this is, all have sinned, all have hurt others, all have been insensitive, and all have not considered others. All have murdered. "Anyone who hates a brother or sister is a murderer."[28]

The heart cannot distinguish between the act of murder and the feeling of murder. When you feel angry at a person because they are loud, and obnoxious, or insensitive, your heart responds with a desire to shut them up and to blow them away. This is murder. Not all will admit this but all feel it. Son, I want men to deal with their heart, for out of the heart, the mouth speaks[29] *and action occurs.*

If you do not deal with murder in your heart, you will act on it. Maybe not physically killing them, but you will act, like getting even by destroying the reputation of the resort or causing problems for the offender and having them thrown out, or banned from the resort. I want people to see that loving your enemies is dealing with your heart, and letting Me lead you by My Spirit in an alternative way of action. I have told you to pray for those who spitefully use you, forgive those who hurt you, bless those who speak against you, and feed your enemy.

All of these things are contrary to the heart of man but are in alignment with the heart of your Heavenly Father. I will help you do this. Man cannot do this on his own. A man cannot change his own heart by discipline or will. Eventually his true motivation and nature will come out. You've noticed that, this week, when after three days, you had had enough. You could not do this on your own. Your true nature came forward. The solution to all these challenges is to be transparent with your feelings with Me, and ask Me to help you love your enemies.

I will give you strength and a different spirit. Holy Spirit will come into that situation and change your heart. You will be changed not by your will but by My Spirit. Love, joy, peace, patience, and kindness are all fruit of the Holy Spirit, not by your own will or action. It is a way I show forth My Glory in man. It is the fruit of abiding in the vine. It is the result of the virtue that flows from Me to you. It will change your heart so you feel different, and you will love your enemies.

Son, abide in Me and I will abide in you. It is a decision to draw your strength from My power, My glory, and My anointing in situations where you could never do this by your own will or desire to act the way you should. I give you strength. Remember I am your strength, I am your strong tower to rise above the situation. I am the rock that is higher than you, and I will place you there above the situation. I am close to the broken hearted, but you must be honest. You must ask for strength and I will provide it.

Son, loving your enemies is much more than an outward act. It is a way of life. It is always giving grace, and not demanding your own way. It is preferring others to yourself. (Do not worry) I will provide. I will not let you be walked on because you are walking in My revelation, and My words, rather than in your own actions and decisions.

In every situation where you feel indignant or angry, in traffic, or in a lineup, in a hotel room, start talking to Me and say, "Dad I feel angry, indignant, whatever. Please help me to love my enemies. Please help me to demonstrate the fruit of the Holy Spirit. Please give me strength to act the right way and to bless those who spitefully use me and say all manner of evil about me. Please be my protection, my shoulder to cry on. Be my rock that is higher than I and I will do this."

Son, if you hate, it will kill you. Your body is not designed to stay with continuous thoughts of injustice. It will simply burn you up from the inside. Son, this is the cause of many ailments both physical and emotional. I want you to be free and whole. I want you to be free from sickness and destructive forces in your body that destroy your organs. That is why I tell you to love your enemies.

Son, let's close this discussion with the challenge. Will you ask for help when you feel indignation or anger at others? Will you ask Me for strength?

Love,
Dad

Personal Journaling Exercise

1. Think of one situation in your life where you interact with others; how could you be more gracious and loving in that situation?

The Goal

2. Ask God what He would say to you about loving your neighbour; write down all that comes to mind.

3. Pray this prayer: "Dad, please help me to love my enemies. Please help me to demonstrate the fruit of the Holy Spirit. Please give me strength to act the right way and to bless those who spitefully use me and say all manner of evil about me. Please be my protection, my shoulder to cry on, and my rock that is higher than me."

CHAPTER FOUR

Family

Fathers and Their Children

Graham Nash of the band Crosby Stills Nash and Young wrote a song called, "Teach Your Children." It's a simple song that simply says to be involved with your children. The Lord exhorts us the same way. In fact He says:

"Fathers, do not exasperate your children; instead, bring them up in the training (nurture) and instruction (admonition) of the Lord."[30]

I love the fact that the first thing He says is "Don't exasperate your children." Exasperate means to provoke them to anger. Don't push their buttons in a very personal way. All too often we as parents do this. We know them very well and we know what will really bug them, and when we want them to do something we use it against them.

In contrast we are encouraged to train them in the instruction of the Lord. I really like the way the King James Version of the Bible translates this verse. It uses the word "nurture" instead of the word "train." It is much more personal. Nurture means to help (something or someone) to grow, develop, or succeed. It focuses on supplying nourishment. A gardener needs to nurture the vines to produce good grapes. Teachers must nurture students to produce creativity. A mother nurtures her baby when she feeds it. It requires very intimate involvement. We are encouraged to nurture our children in the instructions of the Lord. The word "instruction" or "admonition" used here is a very interesting word. It means "warning through teaching." It is focused on improving a person's reasoning ability so they can reach God's solution, for example, by going through His thought process.[31] This is in direct contrast with the historic belief of teaching children to follow the rules. The focus here is on renewing the mind to think the way God does.

The best way to accomplish this is to show your children how God has an intimate relationship with you. Explain how you have daily communication with Him and receive relevant counsel from Him for each day. A simple word of your testimony to your children will inspire them to want to develop a similar relationship with Him.

Relevance in believing in God is a key need of people today. Many have seen so much abuse at the hands of the church. There are so many voices and opinions bombarding them every day from the media and the internet. They just need to hear a simple truth that demonstrates that God is relevant and real and that He wants to be involved in the situations of their lives.

We are encouraged to teach our children who God is, and what He is like. A family is a picture of the Father's heart. A couple who invests in children, raises them up and stays involved in their lives for all their lives, is a picture of how your Heavenly Father wants to be involved in your life. A parent needs to provide, protect, teach, guide and discipline His children. These are all expressions of love, not duty. So it is with our Heavenly Father. He provides, protects, instructs, provides loving attention, listens, and ensures we are going on the right path.

A father is designed to be the head of the household, but he is balanced by the loving attention and correction of his wife. The balance of the two is how a family was designed. Today this model has been deeply impacted by divorce and self-interest. Few parents are as committed to each other as deeply as they need to be. The consistency of a parent's commitment makes a family feel secure and safe more than anything else. Most children today grow up in an ever present fear of divorce. It is the norm in society and as a result the family feels insecure.

The first thing a father must demonstrate is a commitment to both his wife and his family. He must be prepared to sacrifice anything for his family. This means much more than physical death. It means he gives up his desires for theirs, and his playthings for theirs. His time is not his own; his time is his family's. He can never be too busy for his family. He is the rock on which a family depends. He serves his family.

He serves his wife and children. This is the best way for his family to be secure and sound. A father is to be the servant of his family. Remember the Lord says he who wants to be great must be the servant of all.[32] A father demonstrates this to his own family first.

I am greatly impressed by the young fathers I have seen recently. There appears to be a firm grasp of this truth in their lives. My son, Matthew, and my neighbour, Mike, clearly demonstrate these attributes. They prepare meals and take care of their children personally. They do not push off the care of their children to their wives. They are both remarkable examples of their Heavenly Father.

A family depends on a father's stability and must see him as patient, kind, stable, and committed to his wife. A stable father will ensure a stable household. A stable father demonstrates our Heavenly Father's love and consistency. A stable father is God's gift to a family.

I remember a family in one church where I lived, whose boys were really remarkable. They excelled in what they did and just seemed to really have it together. I asked the father what the secret was to his success with his kids. He was the president of an engineering firm so he was a busy man. He simply said consistency. That was a remarkable statement. It was not something I was particularly good at. It always stuck with me that he was a stable, consistent influence on his family. It provided me with a goal to try to achieve.

Now few men can measure up to these expectations. They are afraid, concerned with their job, financially short most of the time, suffer from feelings of sexual inadequacy, and simply don't feel capable of fulfilling the role of being a stable, consistent individual. This is where the Lord comes in. I felt the Lord say this to me:

Son,
I am your strength; I am your strong tower, and I am your help.
I will help you be all you can be and need to be for your family.
Love,
Dad

Few men have seen men who demonstrate these servant heart characteristics. As a result they do not know what such a person looks like and how they are supposed to act in situations. As a result we really need the Lord to guide us and teach us. A father can come to the Lord

The Goal

and simply ask, "Dad, I don't know what to do, or how to respond, please tell me," and He will tell you.

The Lord's Heart is that men be the type of father their family needs. The verse *"come to me when you are heavy laden, take my yoke upon you, for my burden is light"*[33] is not just about our callings. It's about all situations, it is about being a good Dad. Being a Dad is a very difficult job. A man needs to share with the Lord the burden of raising a family. If we don't, we will not likely succeed. We need the Lord to be our strength.

Husbands and Wives

"Husbands, love your wives, just as Christ loved the church and gave himself up for her."[34]

A husband is to love his wife as Christ loved the church. He is to sacrifice his own life for hers. This is a very important element in a Christian life for a man to do. A wife is not required to love her husband. She will love her husband if her husband loves her.

Love has many expressions. Love is affection, support, being consistently patient, and giving. It is not a simple word.

To most men, love has a very narrow meaning, but in the New Testament the original Greek has four different words that are translated as love in English. Each one conveys a different meaning or set of attributes about love. These four Greek words are as follows:

- *Agape* means "Unconditional love, and charity; It is the love God has for His children." Agape is used in the Biblical passage known as the "love chapter," 1 Corinthians 13, and is described there and throughout the New Testament as brotherly love affection, good will, love, and benevolence. Whether the love given, is returned or not, the person continues to love (even without any self-benefit). Agape is also used in ancient texts to denote feelings for one's children and the feelings for a spouse. It can also be described as the feeling of being content or holding one in high regard.

- *Éros* means love, mostly of the sexual passion. The Modern Greek word "erotas" means "intimate love." It can also apply to dating relationships as well as marriage.

FAMILY

- *Philia* means "affectionate regard, friendship," usually "between equals" or loyalty. It is a dispassionate virtuous love, a concept developed by Aristotle. In his best-known work on ethics, Nicomachean Ethics, philia is expressed variously as loyalty to friends, family, and community, and requires virtue, equality, and familiarity. Furthermore, in the same text, philos denotes a general type of love, used for love between family, between friends, a desire or enjoyment of an activity, as well as between lovers.

- *Storge* means "love, affection" and "especially of parents and children." It is natural affection, like that felt by parents for offspring. It is rarely used in ancient works, and then almost exclusively as a descriptor of relationships within the family.[35]

- *Agape* is the word that is used in the verse, "*Husbands, love your wives.*"[36] It is the type of love that brings forth caring, regardless of the circumstance. It is unconditional love. C.S. Lewis recognized this as the greatest of loves, and saw it as a specifically Christian virtue.

The Goal

How a man shows this type of love, is found in the following verses:

"Submit to one another out of reverence for Christ. Wives, submit yourselves to your own husbands as you do to the Lord. For the husband is the head of the wife as Christ is the head of the church, his body, of which He is the Savior. Now as the church submits to Christ, so also wives should submit to their husbands in everything. Husbands, love your wives, just as Christ loved the church and gave Himself up for her."[37]

These three verses have unfortunately been used by men to suppress women and demand submission. This is a complete warping of these verses. To start with the word "submit" in verse 22 is not even in the Greek; in fact, in both times, used (verse 22[38] and 24[39]) regarding wives, it has been added by the translator. The Greek transliteration of verse 21 reads "Submit one to another out of reverence for Christ, wives to your husband." Including the word "submit" twice in verse 22 and in 24, causes the verse to stress the belief that wives must submit and do whatever their husbands say and men do not. It comes across as a command, this is not what it says.

It states simply that both husband and wives are supposed to submit to each other. Now the next question is "what does the word submit mean?" In verse 22 the words "submit to one another" is translated from *hypotáss* (from Strong's 5259 /hypó, "under" and Strong's 5021 /táss , "arrange")—properly, "under God's arrangement." It is a complex word and means different things depending on the context. It can mean "to subject oneself, to obey; to submit to one's control; to yield to one's admonition or advice."[40]

In this case, I believe the words "to yield to one's admonition or advice" is a very good translation in this context. In simple words it means "listen to each other's advice." Love cannot be forced. Wives who are forced to do something against their will, do not feel loved, and it is not the act of a loving husband. Husbands are clearly told to love their wives, so forced submission just does not fit the context.

The language of love for most women are words and communication. Women want to be listened to. Their words and advice are to be treasured. The greatest act of love a man can do sometimes is to simply give their undivided attention to their wives, to listen to them, and heed their advice. When a person is listened to, and their opinion heard and followed, it validates a person. Unfortunately many women feel discounted by their husbands simply because they don't listen to them, or do anything they suggest. Husbands show love to their wives when they listen to them, and value what they say.

This also applies to women. Many men feel not listened to, not appreciated or respected. Many men find it difficult to argue with their wife simply because women seem to remember everything and men do not. As a result men often give up for the sake of peace in their house, and don't argue, but don't listen either.

Men generally want to fix problems and actually don't need to be told something ten times, especially if they really love their wives. They want to fix the situation. It is the nature of man. When a women continues to repeat a request over and over, this will annoy the man. So communication and learning to get it right is complex and takes a commitment on both sides to submit to one another. To yield to each other's admonition and counsel.

Romance

Romance is a critical responsibility that a man must demonstrate to his wife for their entire married life. He must never take her for granted. He must continue to woo her. Romance starts with words that a man says to his wife. It always starts with words. Words that inflate an ego are not romance. Romance is honest, genuine, and sincere. A husband is called to romance his wife and to continually show affection in both deeds and words. Romance is the language of life in a marriage. Without it, it becomes stale and a drudgery.

Love is seen in action, words, and faithfulness. A man is to be the husband of one wife. He is to be monogamous. He cannot have a mistress. Pornography is a type of mistress. Jesus said if a man lusts after a woman he commits adultery with her. If a husband has adultery in his heart, it will colour his relationship with his wife. Their wedding bed will be defiled, because the presence of the other woman in the pornographic picture will be there. Men must demonstrate love for their wives in this area specifically and turn from pornography and from all sexual fantasy. This will only undermine a relationship with their wives.

A man must provide for his wife. Provision starts with our physical needs, of food, water, shelter, and clothing and this is just the start. He

The Goal

must also ensure that he provides a safe home, safe from criminals, safe from loss of all types and safe from financial crisis. He must save for the future. A man must provide for his family including the future. Therefore financially he must manage his funds well. He must save for the future and manage the household finances well. A wife feels insecure and unsafe if the finances of the home are not sound.

A husband must love his children. A wife needs to see this. He must consistently care for them, discipline them, and provide time for recreation for his family. A wife wants her children to be secure, provided for, loved and supported. She does not want to see favoritism or injustice towards her children.

I asked the Lord what He would like to say about this topic. I saw him with a baseball bat getting ready to hit a ball and this what I felt He said to me:

Son,

A family is melded together by love, forgiveness, and activity. A family that plays together is happier. When parents are not involved in their children's play time, children grow up distant, removed from their parents. They do not see why they should be involved as adults with their parents because the never learned to play together when they were children.

A parent may be busy, providing and making ends meet. This is important, but just as important, is playing baseball with a child, and enjoying the things they enjoy. Yes it costs a parent time, and often parents do not feel they have the time, yet it is the best investment of their time.

Husband and wives must also play together. This is a critical activity that many families lose. When a couple first starts dating, they can't wait to be together, to talk, and to play. This often gets lost as a marriage gets older. Playing together is very important and just as with children, marriage relationships are strong when husbands and wives play together.

Love,
Dad

Our Heavenly Father walked in the cool of the evening with Adam and Eve. It was very clear that He built His relationship with his children by spending time with them. Play binds parents to children, and spouses together. I encourage you to make it a priority in your family's life.

Personal Journaling Exercise

1. Ask yourself: "How easy do I find it to listen to my wife/husband, my children, and other family members?" Write down your honest answer.

2. How much time is devoted to spending time with your family? How much should be devoted? Make a decision to rectify this.

3. Ask God what He wants to say to you about your devotion to spouse, children and family. Be still for a while and write down what comes to mind.

CHAPTER FIVE

Abide in Me

"I am the true vine, and my Father is the gardener."[41]

The Lord tells us that He is the vine and His Heavenly Father is the gardener.

A gardener is intimately involved with his vineyard. A vintner cannot produce a great wine without great grapes. It takes a lot of time and nurture to produce great grapes. A gardener needs to watch over the vineyard every day and ensure no weeds take over, no birds eat the fruit, and no blight attacks the vine. He nurtures the process. That's what our Heavenly Father does for us, though we have a key responsibility. We need to stay connected to the vine.

"Remain (abide) in me, as I also remain in you. No branch can bear fruit by itself; it must remain in the vine. Neither can you bear fruit unless you remain in me."[42]

The word *remain* or *abide* simply means, "not to depart, not to leave, to continue to be present, to maintain unbroken fellowship with one, and to be constantly influenced by the Holy Spirit."[43] In other words, we need to stay connected to the Lord.

As I thought of this verse, I considered how a computer abides in a central control system for security patches and feature updates. It can make decisions to some extent on its own but to be fully protected it must abide in the computer's operating system security architecture. This is somewhat like how the Lord wants us to live. We are able to operate on our own but still need to stay connected to the main system for continual updates and protection.

The Goal

The key part of this verse is the continuous connection and the flow of life that the vine provides to the branch to produce fruit. The computer analogy is like a threat warning system. It focuses on protection, and this verse focuses on fruit. The Lord wants His people to produce the fruit of the Spirit. The fruit of Holy Spirit is the goal in a person's life. This is what people demonstrate to others. This is what others see. This is what draws men and women to Christ. The abiding scripture focuses on connection and trust to accomplish this.

In a vine, fruit is the result of the life flowing from the ground, through the root, and through the branch. It is an interesting mixture of the generics of the root system and the genetic structure of the branch. Only working together is fruit produced. Each branch produces fruit after the type of tree it is.

There are nine fruits of Holy Spirit commonly mentioned. They are, love, joy, peace, patience, kindness, goodness, faithfulness, gentleness, and self-control.[44] However these are not the only fruits that Holy Spirit can produce. In the Old Testament Moses assigned the design and construction of the tabernacle to Bezalel and filled him with the Spirit of God and ability in craftsmanship. Here is the verse referring to this individual.

> *"See the Lord has called by name Bezalel, and He has filled him with the Spirit of God, with ability, with intelligence, with knowledge, and with craftsmanship to devise artistic designs, to work in gold and silver and bronze, in cutting stones for setting, and in carving wood, for work in every skilled craft."*[45]

I believe that there can be fruit produced in areas such as creativity, innovation, engineering and relationship. Creativity in the arts is a fruit of Holy Spirit to those who are called to that realm. Wealth creation is the fruit of Holy Spirit for those called to business. Invention is the fruit of Holy Spirit to those called to the science world. Decisiveness is the fruit of the Holy Spirit for those called to government. In each mountain of the world system there is a unique fruit produced by a believer who is called to that realm. The Lord calls men and women to different mountains to be light and salt in the areas where their gifts are best expressed. They will produce the unique fruit that that realm requires. It is the fruit of Holy Spirit. Abiding in the

Lord is the key to producing all fruit. How to abide is the real question for most people.

Abiding is not a one-time decision or choice as often thought. Our daily situations need our heart to be continually connected to the heart of the Lord and to be at one with our Heavenly Father. Jesus said, "I want them to be one just as we are one."46 The concept of unity is the foundation of abiding.

As a branch is grafted into a vine, so we are grafted into the Lord by the cross and the sacrifice accomplished on it. We are integrated into the Father. Our spirit is integrated into Holy Spirit. He dwells in us and we dwell in Him. We are of one heart. The decisions we face each day require a flow from the vine to produce the fruit required. When we are angry, we need flow to produce peace. When we are depressed, we need flow to have joy. When we are confused and hopeless, we need flow to receive wisdom and a willing spirit to continue.

The question we have to face is; "What would our lives look like if we were really abiding in Christ?" What would we accomplish? How would others notice it? What would be the outcome? I asked my home group this question, and some said that we would speak words that encourage, we would pray for others quickly and we would not be afraid to share what God has done for us. I felt if I was constantly abiding in Christ, I would not get uptight when things seem to go wrong, even simple things like waiting on the telephone line for a call centre to answer. I felt I would not get upset with the call person after waiting a long time, and slip into an entitlement mentality. Another member of my group agreed that would be abiding.

I had an opportunity the next day to put that into practice when I called Bell Canada and was put on hold for 1.5 hours. I was feeling really tense, yet I kept saying, "Lord, I want to abide in Christ. Help me, I trust You that You will resolve this problem." After 2 hours from my initial call, the problem was resolved and I had kept my cool. I asked the person I had called where they lived and the call centre person said the Philippines. She said she was sorry that I had to wait so long. They had had a flood in the Philippines and people could not get into work. I asked the Lord to bless her. I was sure glad that I didn't get upset. My problems were insignificant in comparison to the problems they were having. I had accomplished abiding. Yeah!

The Goal

Each situation requires flow from the Lord's vine to produce the correct fruit. Dependency is the critical component; that said, a person can choose not to receive flow, not to ask for flow, and not recognize the need for flow from Holy Spirit, to produce His fruit. All these behaviours are very common. The decision that men must face is, "Will you become dependent on Holy Spirit or just try to produce the fruit of the Holy Spirit on your own?"

I asked the Lord what He would say about abiding and what did the scripture "abide in Christ" mean? This is what I felt He said:

Son,

Abide—this term means to rest in the connection. A branch does not strive to be connected or stay connected. The vineyard gardener graphs the branch in and supports it to stay. So there is no effort required to abide in the vine. It is only a will issue to draw on the resources of the vine to stay connected at the heart level.

A person can appear to be connected, but in their heart they are not. They do not choose to stay connected. They are not dependent on the flow of life from their Heavenly Father. They will not produce fruit and eventually will fall away. These are the branches that are collected and destroyed. However, a person who chooses to remain in Me and I in them, will produce fruit and be the light of the world.

A branch draws on life from the vine. Now when does a vine need to give life to the branch? It is all the time for a branch to live. A branch needs life to be flexible and not be brittle. Without life from the vine, it will die. It becomes brittle, inflexible, and dogmatic. Many people become like this. The Pharisees looked like they were connected to the vine, but they were not. They become harsh, religious, dogmatic, and they put loads on other people telling them that this is how you are to behave or this is how you are to perform. The goal of the Pharisees' appearance was to look like they were connected to the vine even though they were not.

This happens to many of My children. They become dependent not on the flow from the vine but on themselves, on their own righteousness. Their actions are driven by a heart not connected to the vine. The fruit of their branches is not fruit of the Spirit but fruit of their own making. Most of it is harsh, sour and bitter.

Abide in Me

A man must choose to draw on the life of the vine to produce the fruit of the Spirit. This is done by continuously sharing your needs and requests with Me. I will give to all who ask. "You have not, because you have asked not," is a key scripture here. Creating a heart of dependency is the start to flexibility. If you do this, you will naturally produce fruit without asking to produce fruit. It will just come from the flow that comes from Me. You will ask anything in My name and you will receive it.

This Scripture (abide in Christ) means developing a heart that acknowledges that out of your own life you cannot produce the fruit of the Holy Spirit. You need Holy Spirit to produce the fruit of the Holy Spirit. There is no place for self-sufficiency in this situation.

Son, when a person faces a problem at work or in his family or in a relationship, he wants to act. Men want to fix situations. They can act out of their own wisdom or mind or the Lord's. It's a choice. A man needs wisdom when he doesn't know what to do. Now in many things, a person believes they know what to do. Does that mean he has to ask Me if he knows what to do? The answer is yes. If he abides he does not assume he is always right. It is best for man to ask Me for My wisdom to ensure his choices are sound. A man can be easily deceived, particularly in an area where they have knowledge and experience. They assume they don't need God's flow of wisdom in those situations. This is dangerous. Man does not know everything, and deceives himself when he thinks he knows.

Son, a man needs to get into the habit of asking for wisdom each day. A branch asks for flow, every minute each day to live. This is how a man is to live. Abide in me, drink of me, live the life that I give, and you will live continually, producing daily the fruit of the Spirit in your life.

Love,
Dad

The Goal

Personal Journaling Exercise

1. Think of the main arena where you spend your time (e.g. workplace, college, etc.). How could abiding in Him change your approach there?

2. Ask God if there are any areas of self-dependence that you need to yield to Him.

3. Pray the following: "Heavenly Father, thank You that if I abide in You each day I can flourish. Help me to depend on the Holy Spirit each day, so that I might produce fruit in the realm to which I am called. Change me and teach me to do this, that my life may be lived in Your love and for You—amen."

CHAPTER SIX

Honour Your Parents

> "'Honor your father and mother'—which is the first commandment with a promise so that it may go well with you and that you may enjoy long life on the earth."[47]

Honour your father and mother is the first commandment with promise.

I was raised in a home where both my parents honoured their parents, and they all had a long life. My father is 90 and is still with us. My grandfather lived until he was 96. The challenge for us is what does honour looks like. I can think of a few things.

1. Honouring what they did well.
2. Forgiving their mistakes.
3. Speaking well of them.
4. Supporting them in their old age.
5. Serving them when they no longer can take care of themselves.

Many find these things hard to do because of abuse they took from parents when they were growing up, or simple selfishness. Selfishness is very common. Many children cannot bother to stay involved with their parents' lives as they get older. They have too many other things to do. Soon their parents pass away and they cannot visit them because they are gone.

- Honour is a decision to give time even when it is inconvenient.
- Honour means to respect, to attribute value to their words, and to their experience.

The Goal

- Honour is deciding to go the extra mile for a parent even when you don't want to.

- Honour is ensuring their needs are met and health and financial issues are dealt with in a manner that protects their dignity when they no longer can independently function in these areas.

- Honour is being respectful and thankful for their investment in you.

- Honour is being a face of hope as the end draws near, confirming the worth and value of their lives, acknowledging the foundation they have provided for the ongoing generations.

I am greatly impressed by how my sister honours my Dad. She takes him to all his doctor's appointments, she pays his bills and ensures that all the financial issues are paid and dealt with, and she ensures he has new clothes and that his clothes are washed. She honours him by these activities. She also honours our family by these practical demonstrations of a servant's heart. My parents can rejoice, that the values of serving that they demonstrated, have been passed on into the next generation. This is honour.

I recently spoke to a man who was going through the process of settling his parents' estate. He told me that although his family are all Christians, he was completely dumbfounded by their behaviour when it came to dealing with the finances of the estate. There was division, and fighting over who got what. This is an all too common story. In one family that I knew the mother passed away and two of the sisters ganged up on the third sister and did not deal equally with the estate. This led to division and the siblings not speaking to each other for over 20 years. These petty squabbles would break the hearts of their parents if they were still alive. This is dishonouring of their parents' sacrifice and investment in their family. It is dishonouring of their parents' memory and of each other.

Many families have destroyed relationships over petty fights and unforgiveness over issues that are years old regarding estates. Forgiveness and releasing judgments is a key to healing this kind of destruction. In forgiving, you are releasing yourselves and others and when repenting of your judgments of others, you are freeing yourself and others from their behaviours. Unfortunately when many judge their parents and refuse to forgive them, they are destined to become all they disliked and hated.

Personal Journal

I asked the Lord what He would like to say about honouring your parents. This is what I felt He said:

Son,

"Honor your father and mother so you may enjoy a long life," is a promise.[48] *I promised to bless all those who bless others, but those who bless parents, who honour them in word and time, and do not criticize them and forgive them, I will grant long life.*

Parents make mistakes. They have children when they are young. They did not know how to live and how to handle anxiety. They worried they could not provide, and most felt hopelessly inadequate for the job. When you forgive them for their mistakes, you honour them. When you help them when they get older, you honour them. When you provide for them, you honour them. When you lift them up with a word of encouragement, you honour them.

Many forsake their parents when they get older, shuffling them off to a nursing home. They are lonely, afraid and worried. They need love. They need to feel secure in their children's care, and this is honouring your parents.

Son, honour means to respect and to attribute value to their words and to their experiences. When you listen to parents tell you their life experiences, you show honour. Son, honour comes in many forms—providing, listening to, valuing, treasuring and loving parents are all forms of honour.

Honour your parents. They will be gone soon, and you won't be able to. You will only have their memory.

Love,
Dad

The Goal

Personal Journaling Exercise

1. What things hinder your relationship with your parents? Bring these to your Heavenly Father now, forgiving and asking for forgiveness as necessary.

2. Repent of any judgments or criticism you've spoken out about them.

3. Prayerfully decide how to give them the right amount of your time, and ask your Father in Heaven to help you put it into practice and what He would like to say to you about how to honour your parents.

CHAPTER SEVEN

Render unto Caesar

> *"Then Jesus said to them, 'Give back to Caesar what is Caesar's and to God what is God's.' And they were amazed at him."*[49]

Jesus was approached by several religious people who had devised a question regarding paying taxes. This question was designed to trap Him. If He said, "Yes, you should pay the taxes," then He was a friend of Rome. If He said, "No, you should not pay the taxes," then He was in rebellion to Rome. It was a clever scheme to make Him look bad. He responded by showing them a coin, and asking them whose face was on the coin. They replied, "Caesar's." He then replied, "Give back to Caesar what is Caesar's and give to God what is God's"[50] and they were all amazed.

Jesus supported manmade governments and expects us to do so as well. Governments are established by God[51] to rule the people of the world. There is another realm of spiritual power set up in this world as well.[52] There are spiritual principalities that are set up over countries, regions, even cities, and neighbourhoods based on historic rights of the nations. Sin provides these demonic spiritual powers, rights over a region. If there is no sin, there are no rights; unfortunately, the older the country is, the older the rights. Much of the world is ruled by ancient structures set up by centuries of rights that a people have given to the principalities. Fortunately, Christians are not part of this world structure. They are part of the Kingdom of God.

By accepting Christ and His lordship, believers reject a region's demonic ruler and as such there is a war set up, between the believer and the principalities. The principality cannot touch the Christian. The

The Goal

principality is subject to the policies of the Kingdom of God and therefore cannot touch God's anointed.

However, Christians are often slaughtered by the human followers of these principalities. These human followers are driven by vain expectations of reward for committing a murder. Many evil men use religion as a vehicle for committing atrocities to support their addiction to bloodlust.

All this is going on in the world right now, and you see it played out in many regions. God establishes governments to rule with justice and if they do, they will survive. If they do not, they will be replaced. The Lord is in charge of the world. The earth is the Lord's and everything in it.

Behaving righteously is a key responsibility of government and its leaders. We are told to pray for those who are in authority over us[53] and to honour our leaders. We are to pray for our leaders to rule well and that they are not persuaded by an unrighteous influence and that they commit themselves to righteous government.

We are to pay our taxes so they have the funds to manage the programs and governments' costs so the country is healthy and well cared for. Consider countries where taxes are not paid. The country's water systems, and sewage utilities are all poor. Police are corrupt and crime is rampant. The drug lords and the cartels establish the law and lawlessness becomes the norm.

Governments are given the right to execute judgment and to incarcerate lawbreakers. They have the responsibility to do that. Pray that they execute this responsibility well.

A government employee is a servant of the people. Christians should actively become involved in government at all levels. They are called to be servants of all. Government is a very important place for Christians to be actively involved, at all levels. School boards, the municipal, the provincial, and the federal government, are clearly places to be a servant leader and to bring light.

The minister responsible for a government ministry is a critical person of influence and plays a critical role for a believer. The minister sets the tone for his entire ministry. If a minister demonstrates a servant heart, all that ministry will demonstrate it as well. If the minister is a self-serving politician, this behaviour will be manifested in every layer of the administration. It is very difficult for government structure to rise above its leadership. May Christians rise to these positions and operate out of kingdom principles of God's wisdom.

I asked the Lord about this topic. This is what I felt He said to me:

Son,

Greece is failing right now because the citizens refuse to pay taxes. They will bring the downfall of their own economy because of greed. They are sowing unfaithfulness and they will reap anarchy.

Son, I establish government to rule, to protect the people, and to provide for the welfare of the nation. Not all governments are honest, and not all are faithful, but the poorest government is better than no government. If people do not support their governments, they and their families will suffer. "Render unto Caesar" is not just limited to taxes. It also includes time.

I have called many righteous men and women to government but few will go. They do not give of themselves to serve their nations, and provide a righteous government. If the righteous will not give of their time, then the unrighteous will fill the gap and government will be led by those who will choose to lead.

Son, this is the call on my people. Answer the call to government, render not just your taxes but your time, your wisdom, your ideas, and your talent.

Love,
Dad

Personal Journaling Exercise

We have deep responsibilities regarding government if we are to accomplish what Jesus wants us to do. We need to pray for all those in authority, and not belittle them or speak evil of them. We need to pray that men and women of integrity are raised to fill the roles in the government. We must pay our taxes and not cheat in any of our financial dealings. And we also need to be open to any way in which He is calling us to get involved in government ourselves. All these things will enable the Kingdom to come more and more in our nation.

1. Confess any negative or critical attitudes about government to God.

The Goal

2. Do you know who your local leaders are? Find out, put their names in a prominent place, and pray for them daily.

3. Ask God if there is any way you might encourage them. Be still, and write down what comes to mind.

CHAPTER EIGHT

Go the Extra Mile

"If anyone forces you to go one mile, go with them two miles."[54]

When Jesus walked on the earth, a Roman soldier could require anyone to carry their backpack for a mile. This particular verse is related to this practice. People would see this as a great intrusion on their rights and would begrudgingly carry the pack. Jesus challenges this entire premise by saying that if you are compelled to carry the backpack for a mile, go an extra mile. You have to wonder why He said this. I believe it is because He wants us to learn how to live at peace with all men, and even to love our enemies. By going the extra mile, the heart of the one who compelled you to carry the pack, is touched. They know you did not have to do it, but still you do it. People cannot stay hard in the face of grace. The simple act of showing grace even to a hardened Roman soldier would melt his heart. If we go the extra mile for others, we will melt their hearts for the Kingdom of God.

I once had a dream of a boy who smashed my car's rear window and I had to get it repaired. I installed a plastic window and forgave him for smashing the car. He came back and gave us trouble again and he tried to smash the window but he could not, so he smashed the car itself. We called the police but they never seemed to come. We had to spend time with the kid. I did not want to do this. I really did not trust him, and I really didn't like him but I felt challenged by the Lord. Would I love this enemy? I could not sleep so I asked the Lord about the dream and I believe He said this to me:

The Goal

Son,

This dream is about going the extra mile. You know the story of the Roman soldier who required you to carry his pack a mile and if you carried it a second mile, you were doing this on your own. Son, I encourage everyone to go the second mile with all men especially your enemies. Let's talk about why this is important.

An enemy is a person who wants his way or will over yours. In war, they are an agent of the state and can carry the will of the state. Their goal is to disable you from winning. They may kill you to do this. There are other types of enemies. Anyone who wants their way or will over yours, is an enemy against your heart. Family members can become enemies.

Enemies can come in many forms—neighbours, work comrades, competitors, and spouses. All can become your enemies. The first challenge with this, is to recognize the enemy and the way they are trying to force their will on you. A sexual abuser is an enemy and wants sexual gratification. I'm not talking about this type of enemy. You do not give this type of enemy an extra mile. I'm talking about the enemy who wants you to do something reasonable like carry their pack. This is a different kind of demand. They have the right to ask this. An abuser does not have the right to abuse you. The soldier had the right to ask you to carry the pack and you were legally required to do it but when you went the extra mile, the impact was profound and your enemy became your friend. This is loving your enemy.

This is very difficult for man to do. The basic desire of man is vengeance and repayment for some injustice. This leads to bitterness, unforgiveness, and physical ailment. Going the extra mile, releases you from these issues because you choose to give freely. The impact on your heart is freedom from the judgments, and bitterness because it was your will that you complied with, not the enemy's.

Let's consider how this can operate in a daily life. In the dream, the young boy was troubled and was constantly acting out. He wanted attention. He longed for validation, as a human being. Children are often like this. So how do you go the extra mile? First, recognize that their outbursts are not an indication of a challenge to your authority, but a cry for help. Second, stop what you're doing and acknowledge them and give them eye contact. Ask them what they want. If you're able to meet their need, do so. If it needs to be dealt with later, tell them you will do it a bit later and then follow through.

Let's look at some other examples. Assume you are simply playing a game like throwing a ball with a child. Instead of playing for ten minutes, play for twenty minutes. Son just a few extra minutes with a child, will speak volumes of life into their heart.

Let's consider work. Assume your manager requests that you do an extra shift because they are behind. Don't say I don't have to. Go the extra mile to help your employer when they need help. There are also cases when you can go the extra mile for an employer that has to nothing to do with job responsibility. Assume you have the responsibility to pack boxes but not clean up the floor around you. Going the extra mile would be simply cleaning up your work area when you're finished.

Assume you sell one product but see an opportunity for another product that your company sells but you don't get paid to sell it. If you position that product in good light and help facilitate the sale, even though you don't get paid to do so, you have gone the extra mile.

Regarding neighbours, when you cut your grass and you cut your neighbour's as well, you have gone the extra mile. Going the extra mile has everything to do with giving of your time and talent even though you don't have to. It is choosing to be generous with your time and talents. Son, the world would be changed if people would simply go the extra mile.

Love,
Dad

Restaurant Example

We have opportunities every day to go the extra mile. Sometimes it can be very simple. For example, once Sue and I were at a restaurant; it was very busy and the owner was a rough sort of guy who was quite grumpy. He was frazzled by the load of customers. Sue noticed that his corned beef sandwiches were excellent, and after the meal she went to him and said, "Thanks, your food is excellent." Initially he was taken back, he did not know what to make of this act of kindness. He did respond with "Thanks" but it was clearly something he did not hear and I'm certain it had an impact on him for the rest of the day. Saying thanks can be one of the simplest ways we go the extra mile.

The Goal

How Do We Respond?

How we respond to others when we are asked to go the extra mile is something we have complete control over. When asked to do something we don't want to, most of us usually grumble, maybe not out loud but usually in our hearts. Our response to being asked to go the extra mile is a key to being light. If we do things cheerfully, we shine. When we do things grumbly, we don't. Let's consider the Roman soldier request once again. The person asked to carry his backpack could show indignation and defiance in his eyes without using words or he could willingly say "sure." As he walked with the soldier, he could curse the soldier, and wish bad things for him and his family, or he could move in the opposite direction and bless the soldier as he walked with him and carried his backpack. He could ask God to protect him in battle, watch over his family, heal his body, grant him favour with his leadership, and bless him to be promoted. This is what Jesus would actually want him to accomplish.

He states in the Gospel of Luke, *"Love your enemies, do good to those who hate you, bless those who curse you, pray for those who mistreat you."*[55]

This is how we are to act when we are asked to go the extra mile. Bless those who ask us, don't curse them and joyfully go the extra mile.

Personal Journaling Exercise

1. List situations you are faced with at work or with family members where you are required to go the extra mile? Do you do it? If not why not? Do you bless them or curse them?

2. Ask the Lord what He would say to you regarding going the extra mile in these situations. Be still, and write down anything that comes to mind.

3. Remember the chapter on abiding? Ask Him for the strength and awareness to continue to abide even when the extra mile is required.

CHAPTER NINE

Stewardship

"His master replied, 'Well done, good and faithful servant! You have been faithful with a few things; I will put you in charge of many things. Come and share your master's happiness!'"[56]

Introduction

The Lord had a lot to say about our responsibilities. The term that is often used for someone who is responsible is the word *steward*. A steward is someone who protects, or is responsible for money, property, etc. or a person whose job is to manage the land and property of another person. Stewardship is the process of conducting, supervising, or the careful and responsible management of something entrusted to one's care. We are called to be good stewards of the things the Lord has given us; some of these things are time, energy, gifts, talents, and finances. This chapter addresses our responsibilities when it comes to stewardship

Matthew 25 contains two parables describing our responsibilities in the area of stewardship. In the first parable, verses 14 through 29 present a master who gives his stewards responsibility to manage his affairs. The master goes away for a period of time and when he returns he asks the stewards what they did with the money that he gave them. What is interesting about this parable is that the first servant was given five bags of gold to invest, and he returned ten bags of gold to his master and received the exhortation *"Well done, good and faithful servant! You have been faithful in a few things I will put you in charge of many things. Come and share your master's happiness."* The second servant was given two bags and he returned four bags of gold, and he received exactly the same exhortation. The third servant was given one bag of gold and he did not invest it. He simply buried it in the ground and then returned it to his master. The master said, *"Why did you not just put it in the bank? You would have at least received some interest."* What is interesting about this parable is the master did not have a different reward for the person who produced ten bags or four bags—the reward was the same. He was only displeased with the individual who did nothing, who did not try or risk.

I believe this parable has much more to do with all the resources given to us. This story is not just about finances. This parable has to do with how we invest the resources given to us. Do we invest them, or do we do nothing with them? The Lord is our provider, He gives us everything. God provides our finances, our energy, our talents, and the period of time that we live on earth. To each, different measures of all four categories are given.

Time

We only have so much time on this earth. Some produce enormous amounts with the exact same amount time as everyone else. Who makes better use of their time—the person who commits themselves to practicing their musical instrument two hours a day, writes a book, prepares meals for their family, and listens to God *or* the person who spends eight hours in front of the television set or on Facebook, and at the end of the day has nothing to show for it. Well the answer is clear. It is the first person; however, how often do we just simply waste time by sitting in front of the television, and not actually do the things that would produce greater value, like improving our musical capability, writing a poem, drawing a picture, planting a garden, caring for a neighbour, or calling someone to encourage them. We need to be good stewards of our time.

Energy

Each of us have only so much energy in a day. I have found as I have become older, that I have about 8.5 hours of really good energy. In my case it is from about 7 o'clock in the morning, to about 3:30 o'clock in the afternoon. After that time my energy begins to reduce, and often by the evening time I'm tired. So how I spend that 8.5 hours is a stewardship question. Do I waste it by answering hours of email that frankly draws the life out of me, or do I invest the first few hours in learning new technologies and methods that I can explain to my customers?

Is it better for me to invest that energy in writing the seminars and practicing the workshops that I'm responsible for, or do I waste the energy by having imaginary conversations about office politics, or wondering why I was not asked to be involved in some program, or why someone else got that opportunity? All of these types of thoughts burn up energy, so it is a stewardship question.

One day, I was very tired at work and I felt the Lord spoke to me, I felt He said this:

Son,

You do not need to do everything you're asked to do (at work). Don't be afraid to say no. You need to focus on a few things and just say no to all the other things they ask you to do. Son, I want you to be realistic about your energy level. This would give you energy for the things of My Kingdom. Right now you have no more energy left for more important things.

Love,
Dad

Being a good steward of our energy is a critical responsibility.

Talents and Skills

We are all given unique talents or skills. To some it is arts, drawing, painting etc.; to some it is engineering (civil, chemistry, electrical, mechanical, or industrial); to others architecture or systems design. To others it is design, oratory, food preparation, gardening, writing, political leadership, cleaning, music, medical, media, teaching and coaching. The list is endless. We all have talents and skills, and you can detect what talents you have by simply writing down what do you like to do, and what are you good at.

Talents need to be developed. You cannot become a good writer, without writing. You cannot become a good musician without practicing, or a good engineer without school and practical experience. Talents are developed over a lifetime. A good steward is committed to improving his talents and polishing his skills, not hiding them, which is burying them. He is also committed to transferring those talents to others, and being an active mentor to a younger person.

Matthew chapter 5 verse 15 states that we are not to put our light under a bushel, but to *"Let your light shine before others so they may see your good deeds and glorify your Father in heaven."* The Greek word for good deeds here comes from the word *ergo*, the word for work[57] or employment. When we are excellent in our employment, we bring glory to our Father in Heaven. For example, I know a good public speaker; he is very good at explaining complex things. At work he commits to understanding complex problems. It often takes him hours to understand the problem. He doesn't settle for a superficial understanding of the issue. He then writes seminars and workshops that explains how to resolve the problem. These are used to guide companies. He then promotes and delivers these seminars and workshops, and trains others to deliver them as well. That's being a good steward of that gift.

Here is another example, we know a couple that lead worship. They commit themselves to learning new songs. They practice together, and they create musical charts. They offer themselves to other churches and deliver these services. This is being a good steward of their musical gifts

Finances

Lastly let's talk about finances. We are all given a certain amount of financial responsibility. Stewardship in this area has to deal with how we manage the money that we are given. Do we invest wisely? Do we produce a result? Do we give generously, or do we waste it? In the first parable we read, the Lord chastised the servant who did not invest the money wisely, and did not return an increase on the Master's gold. But to those servants that did invest wisely and did produce a return, he gave them more. It works the same in the Kingdom of God. If you prove yourself faithful in a little, He will provide you with more to manage. If you do not prove yourself faithful with a little, He will not likely give you any more, since you haven't shown that you are faithful with what you have.

Let's review our financial responsibilities.

Taxes

Jesus taught that we ought to pay our taxes in Matthew 22:21. It is our responsibility as citizens. See the chapter "Render unto Caesar" for more details on this topic.

Church

One day tax collectors who were coming from the temple demanded that the disciples pay their Temple tax.

> *"After Jesus and his disciples arrived in Capernaum, the collectors of the two-drachma temple tax came to Peter and asked, 'Doesn't your teacher pay the temple tax?' 'Yes, he does,' he replied. When Peter came into the house, Jesus was the first to speak. 'What do you think, Simon?' he asked. 'From whom do the kings of the earth collect duty and taxes—from their own children or from others?' 'From others,' Peter answered. 'Then the children are exempt,' Jesus said to him. 'But so that we may not cause offense, go to the lake and throw out your line. Take the first fish you catch; open its mouth and you will find a four-drachma coin. Take it and give it to them for my tax and yours.'"*[58]

It's clear from this Scripture that it's important to give to the church that you attend. All churches need money to cover their costs and it is also important to cover the cost of a salary for the pastor since a *"Laborer is worth his wages."*[59] So this is a legitimate place to provide financial support. Unfortunately, there has been a lot of abuse and manipulation that has happened in the area of giving in churches. Many feel manipulated into giving or have felt pressure or guilt to give more than they can afford. As a result they become embittered or just leave the church. This is unfortunate. I particularly encourage people to follow the counsel the apostle Paul gives when it comes to giving. He states:

> *"Each of you should give what you have decided in your heart to give, not reluctantly or under compulsion, for God loves a cheerful giver."*[60]

You should never give if you feel guilty, and you should never give out of fear. The Bible tells us, *"There is no condemnation (guilt) for those who are in Christ Jesus."*[61] It also tells us that *"God has not given us a spirit of fear."*[62] Unfortunately people often give out of these two motivations. This is wrong. When it comes to all decisions, the key scripture that should be used to guide your decision is *"Let the peace of God rule in your heart."*[63] If you do not have peace about giving, don't give. If you feel fear, or guilt, don't give.

The truth is, God will not love you any less if you never gave a dime, and He will not love you any more than He loves you right now, if you gave everything you own. He loves you just as you are. Giving is learned over time. I encourage you to decide in your heart what you would like to give, and consistently give this. The consistent giving will help you to grow in giving.

Benevolence

Jesus taught that we should use our financial resources to help the poor and needy through benevolence. This tightly links to loving your neighbour as yourself. Jesus illustrated this by telling the following parable to a religious leader during a discussion about eternal life:

> *"But he wanted to justify himself, so he asked Jesus, 'And who is my neighbour?' In reply Jesus said: 'A man was going down from Jerusalem to Jericho, when he was attacked by robbers. They stripped him of his clothes, beat him and went away, leaving him half dead. A priest happened to be going down the same road, and when he saw the man, he passed by on the other side. So too, a Levite, when he came to the place and saw him, passed by on the other side. But a Samaritan, as he traveled, came where the man was; and when he saw him, he took pity on him. He went to him and bandaged his wounds, pouring on oil and wine. Then he put the man on his own donkey, brought him to an inn and took care of him. The next day he took out two denarii and gave them to the innkeeper. "Look after him," he said, "and when I return, I will reimburse you for any extra expense you may have." Which of these three do you think was a neighbour to the man who fell into the hands of robbers?' The expert in the law replied, 'The one who had mercy on him.' Jesus told him, 'Go and do likewise.'"*[64]

We are to provide for others. In this parable this Samaritan did not even know the person that he was providing for, but he gave anyway.

Family

Jesus taught us that it's important to give to our own families, to not ignore our immediate family in their time of need. There was a practice at the time of Jesus that was called *Corban*. It was a type of offering that a person would give to the Temple. Jesus specifically addressed this because there were certain members of the Temple that were not providing for their immediate family because they were saying they were giving the money to the Temple as Corban. Jesus specifically rebukes this practice in the following scripture:

> *"You have a fine way of setting aside the commands of God in order to observe your own traditions! For Moses said, 'Honor your father and mother,' and, 'Anyone who curses their father or mother is to be put to death.' But you say that if anyone declares that what might have been used to help their father or mother is Corban (that is, devoted to God) then you no longer let them do anything for their father or mother. Thus you nullify the word of God by your tradition that you have handed down. And you do many things like that."*[65]

Jesus clearly tells us to look after our family. The Apostle Paul further tells us, *"Anyone who does not provide for their relatives, and especially for their own household, has denied the faith and is worse than an unbeliever."*[66] The word translated "provide" is a unique Greek word that means "take thought for beforehand, and provide for." I believe that this includes the principle of saving for the future, not just the present.

Principles of Financial Stewardship

Financial stewardship requires us to have good control of expenses, clear visibility of our budget, and committing ourselves to live within our means. You cannot be generous if you do not decide to be generous. The first key strategy for financial stewardship is the establishment of a well-defined budget that specifies how much you plan to save and how much you plan to give. Many are reluctant to do this, preferring to believe that magic will save them, like a lottery. The lottery is not a solution. A good steward understands both his costs, and his income, and takes managing his budget, seriously. There is no other way to ensure that you can accomplish both the saving and giving goals.

Jesus values budgeting and estimating expenses. He stated that we should not build a tower without first determining the expense.[67] Today debt is higher than it's ever been, primarily because the cost of money is so low, and as a result many people have exceeded their ability to repay their bills. Only good budgeting will help a person to plan to save, to give, to pay their bills, and to repay their debts.

Principles of Giving

Giving should not be a reckless act driven by emotional appeal or, worse, driven by a belief that if I give, it will be given to me. God is not coin operated. It is true that if you are a faithful steward, more will be given to you to manage, but to give to get, is not a Biblical principle. Unfortunately it is often presented that way by some people.

Jesus tells us that when we give, do not be like the Pharisees who announce to all that they are giving money. It was common practice at the time of Jesus for the rich to draw attention to themselves when they were giving in the temple so all could see what they were giving. Jesus said in response to this, that they have their reward. Instead, He said, "When you give, don't let your right hand now what your left hand, is doing. Give in secret and then God will reward you openly."

Once Jesus and His disciples were watching people giving at the temple, and after the Pharisee gave his money, a widow came forward and put in her two mites. This was about one penny. Jesus said that the widow gave the most, because she gave all she had.

My mother was raised in poverty. She was raised in the 1930s and her father contracted Bell's palsy and was unable to work as a cheese maker. As a result my grandmother grew most of their food, but during the winter she would run a tab at one of the local grocery stores. My mother told me a story of how my grandmother went to church and put her last nickel on the offering plate. My mother was disturbed because she knew that was the only money my grandmother had. She said to her mother, "How can you put your last nickel on the offering plate?" My grandmother said, "The Lord will provide another nickel next week." I'm grateful for the Godly heritage in my family. I am reminded by this story, of what the Lord considers real value when it comes to offerings.

STEWARDSHIP

Sue and I were ministering in Mozambique one time and I found out that Bill Gates had been investing billions of dollars in Africa. In North America, nobody to seemed to know anything about it. He did not tell anyone—he just did it. His good friend, Warren Buffett, was so impressed at Bill's ability to wisely invest money in good causes, that he gave Bill half his wealth, saying, "Bill you are really good at this. Here, give away half of my money." Bill and Warren also challenged all the billionaires in the USA to give away half their wealth. We need to give in the same way. No one should know when we are giving, to whom we are giving, and how much we give.

I asked the Lord what He would say to us about being a good Steward. This is what I felt He has to say about this topic:

Son,

Giving is an art form. It is not an activity that men should take lightly. I will give you eyes to see needs, and your heart will also feel needs. You need to listen to Me to understand which needs to give to. Not all needs should be met—some giving is wasteful, irresponsible, and some giving is done to please men. None of this type of giving is of value. Only wise investment of your hard earned money is what a steward should consider. A good steward expects a return on his investments, so you should consider this when you give. I have many people who are investing their hard earned wages in foolish enterprises because of guilt. They also do not look seriously at the results of the investment. No good steward does this. They look seriously at the person they are giving to, or the institution they are investing in, and ask themselves, "If this were a commercial investment, would I invest in this?" My people should ask Me if they should invest in a ministry, or in any need. I will tell them, I do not want My people to waste their money, I want them to have funds to live on, to give away, and to have for their old age. I will bless wise giving, but I cannot bless poor giving. A good steward is a wise investor; my children must become wise. If any man lacks wisdom, let him ask of Me and I will give it to them.

Love,
Dad

The Goal

Personal Journaling Exercise

1. Are you budgeting and developing a plan that will enable to plan, to save, and to give?

2. Are you making the best use of your time, energy, and talents?

3. Ask the Lord what He would like to say to you about being a good steward.

CHAPTER TEN

Leadership

"Whoever desires to become great among you, shall be your servant. And whoever of you desires to be first, shall be slave of all. For even the Son of Man did not come to be served, but to serve, and to give His life a ransom for many."[68]

The Lord specifically tells us go into all the world and preach the gospel. Lance Wallnau has described the world as having seven mountains.[69] These seven mountains represent the seven different realms of power in the world. They include:

1. Government and Law
2. Media and Communication
3. Education
4. Family/Community/Society
5. Business and Finance
6. Spirituality and the Church
7. Arts and Entertainment

We are called to be light in all of these realms. I know I'm called to the business realm; others are called to different realms. The economies of the world are failing due to poor management, poor politically driven decisions, and because we do not have enough wise leaders. The world needs people to be leaders in all these realms, leaders whose motivation is not self-interest but that of a servant.

The Goal

Jesus talked about the true characteristics of a leader when He spoke to His disciples:

> *"But Jesus called them [his disciples] to Himself and said to them, 'You know that those who are considered rulers over the Gentiles, lord it over them, and their great ones exercise authority over them. Yet it shall not be so among you; but whoever desires to become great among you, shall be your servant. And whoever of you desires to be first, shall be slave of all. For even the Son of Man did not come to be served, but to serve, and to give His life a ransom for many.'"* [70]

Most leadership approaches have a top-down, hierarchical style. Servant leadership, in contrast, emphasizes collaboration, trust, empathy, and the ethical use of power. At the heart of this leadership style is an individual who is a servant first, who makes the conscious decision to lead in order to better serve others and not to increase his own power. Their objective is to enhance the growth of individuals in their organization, increase teamwork and personal involvement. A recent behavioural economics experiment demonstrated the group benefits of servant leadership. "Teams of players coordinated their actions better with a servant leader resulting in improved outcomes for the followers (but not for the selfless leaders)."[71]

I met a man in Belgium who had a PhD in economics. He was a wonderful believer. He was clearly called to solve world economic problems. He was not just a professor at a university; he had the potential to be the light to the world in the area of Economics. He also had a deep commitment to being a servant leader.

Our world needs servant leaders. When we lead as a servant, we are light.

The Lord wants His people involved in the world, but we are called to be light to the world as well as to the church. The world needs to be shown the right way to make decisions. Ethics now needs to be taught because there is little light. In my firm, there is a yearly requirement to do a course on the standards of business conduct. This course focuses on teaching ethics and honesty. This is required because so few seem to understand what is right and wrong and, as a result, need to be taught basics things like don't lie, don't misrepresent yourself or our products and don't accept a bribe. Few are standing up and saying this is right and this is wrong. The world needs this type of counsel; they need this guidance.

The world needs God's people involved in world issues and problems. All too often God's people withdraw to their churches and do not involve themselves in the world. Clubs are like this. Churches should not be. In clubs, people withdraw to their protected groups of friends and do not get involved with others. The Lord did not live like this. He went where the lepers, prostitutes and tax collectors lived, and talked with them and healed them. This is how we are to be the light of the world. We are to be involved in the world. Now you might say, "This is too hard for me. I can't do this. I don't really think I can be light." Be at peace. You are not designed to do this alone. You are designed to do this with your Heavenly Father. Together, you are partners in being the light of the world, and He doesn't expect us to do it alone. The Bible tells us:

> *"Come to me, all you who are weary and burdened, and I will give you rest. Take my yoke upon you and learn from me, for I am gentle and humble in heart, and you will find rest for your souls. For my yoke is easy and my burden is light."*[72]

The imagery here is of two oxen who are joined together at the neck with a piece of wood called a yoke. It is perfectly designed to help each of the two animals pull their weight when plowing a field. There are different sized animals so the yoke needs to be made to uniquely fit each animal. So it is with us. The Lord wants us to work with Him to bring light into the world. Our part is designed specifically for us. We are not designed to do it on our own. We are to be joined together with the Lord to accomplish His common goals.

The Lord wants His people to join with Him willingly and wear the yoke that is designed for us, and together we work to bring light into the world. He has called men and women to all facets of this world—business, medicine, politics, theatre, and all other fields of endeavour in the realms. In these realms, they will meet many people who are not believers, and who actually do not know anything about God. Their lives will be touched by the words and actions you will bring to them. When we live our lives operating out of God's kingdom culture, we will often operate in a manner contrary to the world, and the world is surprised, and refreshed as they see God's goodness brought into situations.

The Goal

Example of Servant Leadership: Nehemiah

Nehemiah is an exceptional example of being a servant leader. He was the cupbearer to the king of Babylon when he received a message that Jerusalem was in ruins. He was deeply moved by this loss and decided to act. He asked the King of Babylon to help him rebuild Jerusalem. This took great courage, yet he did it. He changed his community and his country because of his actions. We are called to do the same. We can learn from Nehemiah's prayer to the Lord as we face the challenge of Leadership. Here is what he prayed.

> *"Give your servant success today by granting him favor in the presence of this man. I was cupbearer to the king."*[73]

Communities need wisdom help and leaders. God's people are leaders and their ability to hear from God is a key capability that equips them for this role. Communities need a catalyst who will organize them to accomplish tasks. Action is required to solve problems not talk alone. Communities need people to lead, to motivate, to inspire, and to coordinate them to action.

Governments are designed to do this but they cannot do it alone. Their job is to create order out of chaos. Chaos is the lack of leadership, and in countries where strong leadership and coordination are not present, evil abounds. Evil exploits chaos and leaders who are ungodly, will rise up to fill the vacuum left in these situations. Christians must rise up and take their place in leadership in communities; starting with school boards, town councils, and at municipal, provincial, and federal levels of government.

In my community a Pastor of a local church is responsible for the community improvement program. He has been responsible for improving the businesses of our community and creating the downtown core to become a beautiful place to visit. He has instigated many community building events. He recently started a town wide candlelight Carol walk which is bringing people together out into the community in families and allowing a public celebration of Christ's birth. He is a catalyst for change. He is light. Another man in my community heard from God and bought an old house. He had the house torn down and a youth centre built. He was the catalyst for change. He is light.

Leadership

The Lord gives man responsibility to manage the earth, and to rule it. This requires leadership. Whether it's a simple county seat or a prime minister, it requires leadership. It is difficult to face the responsibilities required to do the job. It requires sacrifice of time and often money. It is often a thankless job. Many will criticize and complain. Many will rise up and try to destroy the good work that good leaders do, yet they will not succeed.

Leaders must be quick to forgive, not judge, and always be gracious. The Lord has called us to be leaders in business and other realms, and in the realm that we are called to, we will have strong ability to see the ideas, the future, and how to be a leader. This is a gift, leaders have. They see how to get to where the community needs to go. They can clearly understand the tasks that need to be done, they can assign work, and hold others accountable for these tasks. They will do this without being a harsh taskmaster.

Nehemiah demonstrated this. He saw the needs, secured the political support, and estimated the resources required to complete the task. He coordinated the people, assigned the work, scheduled the labor, addressed the problems, and the project was finished quickly and done well. This is what a Godly leader does. He is deeply involved; he addresses problems head-on and does not sweep them under the rug. He ensures people that issues are addressed and provides the required facilities. He is a peacemaker when the roll is required; he ensures that the quality of the end result is perfect, and ensures that no slothful workmanship is done in his projects.

We close this section by talking about a young woman in our church, who chose to lead and utilize an empty space in a shopping mall to bring God's love to people last Christmas. Our church already had been given permission to use an empty store as a youth drop-in centre, and over 5,000 youth have dropped in and played video games; they've had a safe place to hang out, to chat and to experience a Godly atmosphere of love. This young woman went further, and created a gift wrapping centre last Christmas in an adjoining empty space to the youth area. People came in to have gifts wrapped, have a coffee, hang out and talk about issues. As a result, many received prayer, prophetic words, and healing. This is a very brief description of an undertaking that has had an incredible impact on a mall in a poor area of our city.

The Goal

Because of her leadership, needs are being met, hearts are spiritually changing, doors are opening wider, and the body of Christ is having more opportunity to touch lives; all because of her decision to lead and bring love and service to the mall.

Being a leader is a thankless task at times. A lonely place. Leaders need God. He is close to all men who call on Him, but He is especially close to leaders who call on Him.

I talked with the Lord about leadership. This what I felt the Lord said.

Son,

Leadership is not a place for the timid. It requires a decisive position in many cases. It demands excellence and no compromising is acceptable. Leaders lead by demanding the same things of themselves. Excellence in all they do. Excellence is difficult. It is easy to provide the image of activity without the product of accomplishment. Leaders focus on accomplishment and lead teams and themselves to accomplish, to produce excellent products, to pay attention to detail and to not allow poor quality to escape or be acceptable. Leaders pay attention to details. Son, I know you do this. That's why you are a strong leader.

Love,
Dad

The Lord wants us to succeed. Teams want to succeed, but they need leaders. The Lord will give us the wisdom and season our efforts with grace. It is our responsibility to decide to lead.

Personal Journaling Exercise

1. Is there a situation where you think something needs to happen? Write down your thoughts and vision for that.

2. What could you do to get the vision happening? Listen to God by being still and writing down what comes to mind.

3. Many Biblical leaders were afraid and even disobedient at first (e.g. Gideon, Moses, Jonah, Peter) but then were still used to achieve great things by God. Do you have any fears or worries about carrying out your vision? Bring those to God and ask for the strength to stand up and step in.

CHAPTER ELEVEN

Seek the Kingdom of God

> *"But seek first his kingdom and his righteousness, and all these things will be given to you as well."*[74]

Jesus talked about the Kingdom of God eighty times in the Gospel. It was a critical message that He wanted us to understand. He illustrated what the Kingdom of God was like and how its principles and precepts would be facilitated in our daily decision making. It was His Heart that we would understand these principles and ideas and then use the wisdom and creative ability He has given us, to accomplish those principles. We were never designed to be robots that blindly follow a set of programming rules. We were designed be like Him. We have free will. We are expected to make decisions and use creativity to accomplish the goals of His kingdom.

I recently visited a community that had been designed from the beginning to be a perfect community. All the houses were beautiful and had porches; everything from the street signs to the sewer covers were perfectly designed to match the image of the designer. There were strict rules regarding how things should appear even down to the types of flowers that had to be in your gardens. This kingdom looked beautiful but it did not have the freedom of choice. It also did not have room for personal creativity. It was a kingdom of rules. The Kingdom of God is not like that. It is a celebration of personal creativity.

Our Heavenly Father is the God of creativity. Every snowflake is different, every meadow is covered with flowers and there are millions of different flowers and plants that express his creativity; so it is to be in His Kingdom. We are to be instruments of creativity. He will continually give us creative ideas, and communicate with us but we are expected to use

The Goal

our own creativity and abilities to facilitate those ideas. This is how His kingdom was designed to operate.

What Is a Kingdom?

The concept of kingdom is actually a foreign idea in most countries today. A kingdom is simply a place where a King rules. It is the realm of his influence, where his values, laws and enforcement are in operation. The King is the ruler and his government and subjects follow his rules and values. In an earthly kingdom, a king rules the outward appearance and activities of his subjects. The Kingdom of God is different because it focuses on the heart of a person and is demonstrated in three ways. These ways are as follows:

1. The Kingdom of God is near or at hand.

> *"Repent, for the kingdom of heaven is near."*[75]

The Kingdom of God is near, or at hand. This simply means that we can choose to step into His Kingdom at any time, and ask Him to help us live in that kingdom. Each day we face decisions whether we choose to live by His principles or not. When we choose His ways, and His principles, we step into His Kingdom.

2. The Kingdom of God is within you.

> *"Nor will people say, 'Here it is,' or 'there it is,' because the kingdom of God is within you."*[76]

The Kingdom of God is within, as much as you choose to let Him rule in your decisions and let Him into the closed doors of your heart. All men have parts of their heart where God stands at the door and knocks. He wants to bring His kingdom into those closed doors of injury and past sins, and bring healing, forgiveness and restoration. We have to answer the door to let Him in. He will bring His light, love and healing if we let Him.

3. The Kingdom of God has come upon you.

> *"But if I drive out demons by the Spirit of God, then the kingdom of God has come upon you."*[77]

Jesus made this statement when He was confronted by religious leaders who said, *"It is only by Beelzebub, the prince of demons that this fellow drives out demons."*[78] Jesus responded to this challenge by saying, *"A house divided against itself would fall. So how can Satan throw out Satan?"* He then went on to say that when He casts out demons, the Kingdom of God comes upon you.

Jesus' message was all about the Kingdom of God. His ministry was the illustration of the Kingdom of God. There is no sickness in the Kingdom of God. There is no death in the Kingdom of God. There is only life. When He prayed for the sick or cast out demons, He illustrated His rule in those situations. He took dominion over the sickness, and over the demons and commanded them to leave because He is the King and the sickness and the demonic have to obey. They have no place in His kingdom. We are called to do the same thing. We are called to illustrate that the Kingdom of God is here. When we pray for the sick and when we cast out demons, we are illustrating the Kingdom of God is here. When we do this, we are the light of the world just as Jesus was.

Sue and I have noticed that God's kingdom will manifest as a sphere of influence in a physical space when His power is manifested, and as a result, healing often occurs. People actually feel the presence of God on their skin. At times, we can feel power literally flowing down our arms, as the Kingdom of God is manifested on an individual.

We have also noticed that often miracles seem to increase as testimony is given. The Bible says, *"Faith comes by hearing and hearing by the Word of God"*[79] and *"We overcome him by the word of our testimony."*[80] As testimony is given, the Kingdom of God also comes upon us to do the work of the kingdom.

Jesus continually demonstrated the Kingdom of God in His life. He illustrated the Kingdom of God when He healed the sick, cleansed the lepers, set the demonic free, raised the dead, spoke life to the downtrodden prostitute, spoke acceptance to the woman at the well, restored Peter when he sinned, acknowledged Thomas' lack of faith and offered His hand to put his fingers in the holes of His hands to build up his faith. He demonstrated His authority and power over this world and its government structures, the spiritual world and all the demons and Satan himself, and all nature; for example, He caught a fish to get a coin to pay His taxes and He rebuked the storm.

The Goal

Paul also demonstrated the Kingdom. He said: "*My message and my preaching were not with wise and persuasive words, but with a demonstration of the Spirit's power, so that your faith might not rest on men's wisdom, but on God's power.*"[81]

We are called to do the same. Jesus said:

"I tell you the truth, anyone who has faith in me will do what I have been doing. He will do even greater things than these, because I am going to the Father."[82]

"After this, Jesus traveled about from one town and village to another, proclaiming the good news of the kingdom of God. The Twelve were with him, and he sent them out to preach the kingdom of God and to heal the sick."[83]

I encourage you to test the Kingdom of God by praying a simple prayer if you are not well. Pray this prayer: "This healing belongs to me, because of what Jesus has done. I receive my healing now, in Jesus name."

Test how you feel and see if you feel better. If you do, the Kingdom of God has come upon you.

I asked the Lord what He would like to say about the Kingdom of God. This is what I felt He said.

Son,

The kingdom of God is love, righteousness, and perfection. It is not a rules-based kingdom based on people mindlessly following a prescribed set of laws. This is not what I created man to do. I created man to use his mind to bring light into all aspects of the world, to listen to Me and to work with Me to accomplish this.

The Kingdom of God is the heart of My message. I want my people to be the executors of My laws and precepts, not by being harsh bosses but by being leaders. Leaders lead. They don't beat people into submission, they inspire and show the way. They are light.

The kingdom of God has rules, principles, and policies that guide decision-making in daily situations. I expect my people to understand My principles and commands and to apply them to daily situations. I expect them to use their mind and say how these principles or commands can be facilitated in each situation.

Son, the rule of any kingdom works this way. No king can be involved in every decision. A good king consistently executes the role of developer of good policy and commands that guide those under him in decisions that need to be made. This is how a kingdom is well-managed.

In My kingdom, I lay out the principles and commandments in the Bible, and I expect My people to read them and know them. I want them to ask Me for wisdom on how to execute these principles. I want them to ask for clarification if they do not understand them.

Love,
Dad

Closing: The Challenge

In closing there are three challenges we would like you to consider:

1. Read the Bible

The apostle Paul gave a challenge to a young man named Timothy. This challenge is as follows:

> "Do your best to present yourself to God as one approved, a worker who does not need to be ashamed and who correctly handles the word of truth."[84]

Paul encouraged Timothy to understand the Bible because *"All Scripture is God-breathed and is useful for teaching, rebuking, correcting and training in righteousness, so that the servant of God may be thoroughly equipped for every good work."*[85] It's important to know what the Bible says, in this way you will not be led astray by people who teach incorrect things.

The apostle Paul talks about a specific group of people in the book of Acts. The author of the book of Acts says they were very noble people. He states: *"Now the Berean Jews were of more noble character than those in Thessalonica, for they received the message with great eagerness and examined the Scriptures every day to see if what Paul said was true."*[86] I encourage you to become like the Bereans and search the Scriptures read the words of Jesus.

Appendix B contains all the commandments that we have been able to find that Jesus wants us to accomplish. I encourage you to read them. Appendix C contains all the Scriptures regarding the Kingdom of

God and of the Kingdom of Heaven that are in the New Testament. We have sorted these by eight categories and we encourage you to read and study these as well.

2. Listen to God

Jesus is our model. He said, *"I am the light of the world."* He also said that you are the light of the world. A key characteristic of Jesus life was that He continually listened to Heavenly Father. Jesus said, *"Very truly I tell you, the Son can do nothing by himself; he can do only what he sees his Father doing, because whatever the Father does the Son also does."*[87] We believe that for us to be the light of the world we must also live following Jesus' example: constantly listening to God, constantly responding to His voice. Constantly asking questions and listening to His answers. We recommend that you practice and develop this lifestyle to accomplish this. Appendix D describes in detail how to hear the voice of God and how to develop a daily lifestyle journaling and hearing God.

3. Do the Work of the Kingdom

James the apostle wrote in his letter a very profound statement. This statement is as follows:

> *"What good is it, my brothers and sisters, if someone claims to have faith but has no deeds? Can such faith save them? Suppose a brother or a sister is without clothes and daily food. If one of you says to them, 'Go in peace; keep warm and well fed,' but does nothing about their physical needs, what good is it? In the same way, faith by itself, if it is not accompanied by action, is dead."*[88]

This is a very deep challenge; it clearly states that if we are really changed by Christ it will be evidenced in the way we live, that we cannot be just hearers of the word, we need to be doers of the word as well. We recommend that you consider ways that you can be light in the world. The Lord will inspire you with you with ways to do it but you have a choice whether you will do it or not. We encourage you to do it.

We have also noticed that God doesn't seem to give new mandates or orders until we finish or at least get started on the things He has already asked us to do. We have felt that we have entered a season where all should do the things that God has asked us to do. We may have to finish the unfinished and create what has been on our hearts for years. We all know that there is great blessing in obedience so we need to challenge ourselves. We need to ask ourselves why we haven't written or recorded the songs, written the books or pamphlets, done the paintings, built the businesses, visited the Nursing homes, had the neighbourhood party, or acted on the reoccurring ideas that have continued to be dropped in our hearts for years. The only answer is that we let other things become more important. The tyranny of the urgent often overrides the important. Don't let busyness, fear, insecurity and lack of resources keep you from recognizing the ideas and projects with your names on them. Don't forget or ignore the invitation God has given you to change the world. In Exodus 35:10 and Exodus 35:30-35, the artists who worked on the Ark of the Covenant and Tabernacle are named alongside the kings, and warriors and prophets. Our Heavenly Father does not say some jobs are more important than others. Each of us is called to do unique things in His kingdom and to bring light into unique places.

You are designed for such a time as this…You are light in the world.
Love,
BILL AND SUE

Action items

1. Ask yourself. "If I could trust in the Lord's provision what would I do for the Kingdom of God, so I could be the light of the world?" Record these thoughts.

2. Write a list of your gifts and abilities and how they have been used for the Kingdom of God…or buried. Perhaps ask a friend what they gifts they see in you.

3. Ask the Lord what He would like to say to you regarding these things you've written down, and what steps you could take to start to move towards accomplishing your heart's desires and using the talents you have been given, to be the light of the world. Listen for a while, then write down what comes to mind.

APPENDIX A

Making Disciples

The Lord wants us to have a wonderful life that has purpose, meaning and fulfillment. Here are five things I believe He wants for us.

Life

John 10:9 *"I am the gate; whoever enters through me will be saved. He will come in and go out, and find pasture. The thief comes only to steal and kill and destroy; I have come that they may have life, and have it to the full."*

Joy

John 15:11 *"I have told you this so that my joy may be in you and that your joy may be complete."*

Peace

John 16:33 *"I have told you these things, so that in me you may have peace. In this world you will have trouble. But take heart! I have overcome the world."*

Fulfillment

Psalm 37:4 *"Delight yourself in the LORD and He will give you the desires of your heart."*

Prosperity

Jeremiah 29:11 *"For I know the plans I have for you, declares the Lord, "plans to prosper you and not to harm you, plans to give you hope and a future."*

The Goal

I believe there are some conditions to these promises. These conditions have to do with how we live, because God cannot bless us if we do not live the way He told us. It is not about our salvation. We are saved by grace, but we are to live by His commandments.

Jesus's last words sum up what He wants us to accomplish. Here is what He said:

> *"Then the eleven disciples went to Galilee, to the mountain where Jesus had told them to go. When they saw Him, they worshiped Him; but some doubted. Then Jesus came to them and said, 'All authority in heaven and on earth has been given to Me. Therefore go and make disciples of all nations, baptizing them in the name of the Father and of the Son and of the Holy Spirit, and teaching them to obey everything I have commanded you. And surely I am with you always, to the very end of the age.'"*[89]

What Is a Disciple?

A disciple is a learner (a true Christ-follower). The Lord wants us to help others become learners, to help someone to progressively learn the Word of God to become a mature, growing disciple (literally, "a learner"). It involves training them in the truths of Scripture and the lifestyle required, and sharing your life with them. It requires a personal investment of time and energy.

> *"The term* disciple *is derived from the Koine Greek word* mathetes, *which means a pupil (of a teacher) or an apprentice (to a master craftsman), translated to English by way of the Latin* discipulus *meaning a learner while the more common English word is student. A disciple is different from an* apostle, *which instead means a messenger."*[90]

Discipleship is the process of becoming like Jesus Christ. It is about growing and maturing, examining and changing the way people think, feel and act.

The concept of a master craftsman and apprentice model is an example of discipleship. A violin master builder teaches an apprentice to design and build violins. It takes a great deal of time to instill the excellence required to build great violins. It requires the Master to inspect all parts of the process and the product produced, and provide continuous coaching. It takes a great deal of time on behalf of the Master builder. So it needs to be for us. When we invest in others it takes time, and attention to a person's life.

We disciple others by personally helping them make better decisions. Investing yourself in another, takes a sacrifice of time.

The Vision

Recently the Lord gave me a vision. I was in an orchard, and it was full of fruit trees, each tree was bearing fruit. He told me that this was a picture of my life, and my ministry. Then He took me to a new small tree that He had just planted. He had a watering can, and He said, "This is a new tree, a new area of your life, this is the tree of developing other ministries."

Very soon after this, I was asked for material that I had developed to help another ministry grow their ministry. I had to decide at that moment if I would hold onto my material or whether I would share it. It was a heart decision. God wants us to develop others to makes disciples but we have to give of ourselves to do it. I gave them the material.

Our Mandate

We are called to help others live out their purpose on earth to have meaningful impact in the spiritual, social and physical needs of communities worldwide.

Here are just a few things we can do:

- Help promote reconciliation
- Equip servant leaders
- Assist the poor
- Care for the sick
- Educate the next generation

Here is an excellent video on what it means to make disciples:

http://www.youtube.com/watch?v=oJWkQ9UP_m8

APPENDIX B

Biblical References of What Jesus Wants Us to Accomplish

What Is a Commandment?

Jesus gave us commandments, directions, and rules for all kinds of situations that help us understand what the Kingdom of God looks like in real life situations. Once He was asked, "What is the greatest commandment?" He responded:

> *"Jesus replied: 'Love the Lord your God with all your heart and with all your soul and with all your mind. This is the first and greatest commandment. And the second is like it: Love your neighbour as yourself. All the Law and the Prophets hang on these two commandments.'"*[91]

This commandment deals with our hearts. If we have this commandment in our heart, we will do the other things He has commanded.

Jesus has given us guidelines and direction on what we are to accomplish in our lives and in this world in our lifetime. The great commission takes on a much greater impact on our personal behaviour on a daily basis. If we consider that Jesus wants us to use our mind to creatively fulfill a set of outcomes in this world, it is much different than blindly following a set of rules.

Jesus used this word "command" again in another verse:

> *"As the Father has loved me, so have I loved you. Now remain in my love. If you keep my commands, you will remain in my love, just as I have kept my Father's commands and remain in his love. I have told you this so that my joy may be in you and that your joy may be complete."*[92]

The Goal

The word *commands* comes from the same Greek word "to accomplish." Jesus is telling us that the true key to joy in our life is to commit to accomplish the things He has given us to do.

It has always been the downfall of the Lord's church to fall into the trap of following laws. Laws are easier than relationship. Laws don't require honesty in your heart. Law only looks to obedience not motive.

The Lord is concerned with the character of the heart of man. He is concerned about developing a heart motivated by love and purity of purpose not self-elevation or self-promotion. Law in contrast leads to pride.

Hearts that are changed by the Lord have several characteristics. First they are humble. They are not self-promoting. They do not try to show their ways are always best. They do not have to be right. They can let others win. They can prefer another over themselves, without feeling they are a second-class citizen. They long to serve not out of duty but out of love. If we are bound by the law, we may serve, but not from a pure heart, not from the heart of love. It is out of a haughty heart that draws self-worth from obedience. "Look at me. I accomplish the rules. Aren't I good?"

The Pharisees were driven by this thinking. The Pharisees wanted to follow the law so they could raise up their value in their own heart and in the eyes of others.

> "The Pharisee stood by himself and prayed: 'God, I thank you that I am not like other people—robbers, evildoers, adulterers—or even like this tax collector.'"[93]

The pure heart does not need to do this. It is secure in the Father's love. It does not envy or look for its own needs to be fulfilled. It does not want to be first. It understands the last is to be first.

Let me tell you an example of a person who has really embraced the concept of accomplishing what Jesus would like us to do. She has clearly become the light of the world in her community. She was a single mother who had a difficult marriage and little education. She unfortunately went through a divorce and had no skills to make a living. She had a choice. She could become bitter or she could accomplish what Jesus wanted. She got a job and went back to school and after many years she graduated as a nurse. She built a home for her family and then she began to change the world. She was a home nurse and noticed that a great deal of medical equipment that was perfectly useful was discarded. She asked if she could harvest this equipment and send it to Mexico to help clinics there that had nothing. She was granted the right to harvest this equipment and as a result of her sensitivity she is now changing the medical conditions of outlying areas of Mexico. Her view of the world also impacted her children. Her youngest daughter at the age of 12 noticed that there was no good equipment in the playground for children in her community. She began to sell cupcakes to raise money and within a short period time raised enough money to pay for all the new playground equipment in her community.

They did not do this because they were following the law. They did this because their hearts were moved by the Lord's heart. They did this because their hearts and, their motivation, was pure and it created the outward behaviours. Character is what the Lord wants to develop. He wants us to have a heart that is compliant with His Heart, and His way of thinking. Jesus gives us many examples on how He thinks on many topics and how the situations would be different if we followed His way of behaving in those situations. He outlines the impact on us and others in the world if we do what He commands.

Now let's look at the specific commandments that Christ gave us so we would know what the Kingdom of God looks like in real world situations.

1. Be the Light of the World

Confess Christ before men—Matthew 10:32-33

Therefore everyone who confesses Me before men, I will also confess him before My Father who is in heaven. But whoever denies Me before men, I will also deny him before My Father who is in heaven.

Make Disciples of all Nations—Matthew 28:19,20

Therefore go and make disciples of all nations, baptizing them in the name of the Father and of the Son and of the Holy Spirit, and teaching them to obey everything I have commanded you.

Be salt and light to this world—Matthew 5:13-16

You are the salt of the earth; but if the salt has become tasteless, how can it be made salty again? It is no longer good for anything, except to be thrown out and trampled underfoot by men. You are the light of the world. A city set on a hill cannot be hidden; nor does anyone light a lamp and put it under a basket, but on the lampstand, and it gives light to all who are in the house. Let your light shine before men in such a way that they may see your good works, and glorify your Father who is in heaven.

Give to him who asks of you, and lend to those who want borrow from you—Matthew 5:42

Give to him who asks of you, and do not turn away from him who wants to borrow from you.

Judge not that you may not be judged—Matthew 7:1-5

Do not judge so that you will not be judged. For in the way you judge, you will be judged; and by your standard of measure, it will be measured to you. Why do you look at the speck that is in your brother's eye, but do not notice the log that is in your own eye? Or how can you say to your brother, 'Let me take the speck out of your eye,' and behold, the log is in your own eye? You hypocrite, first take the log out of your own eye, and then you will see clearly to take the speck out of your brother's eye.

Demonstrate God's Power—Mark 16:17

And these signs will accompany those who believe: In my name they will drive out demons; they will speak in new tongues.

2. Love the Lord

Love God—Matthew 22:37-38

And He said to him, "YOU SHALL LOVE THE LORD YOUR GOD WITH ALL YOUR HEART, AND WITH ALL YOUR SOUL, AND WITH ALL YOUR MIND." This is the great and foremost commandment.

Appendix B: Biblical References of What Jesus Wants...

Hear Gods Voice—Matthew 11:15

Whoever has ears, let them hear

Ask in Faith—Matthew 21:21-22

And Jesus answered and said to them, "Truly I say to you, if you have faith and do not doubt, you will not only do what was done to the fig tree, but even if you say to this mountain, 'Be taken up and cast into the sea,' it will happen. And all things you ask in prayer, believing, you will receive."

Keep alert and watch for the 2nd coming—Matthew 24:44

For this reason you also must be ready; for the Son of Man is coming at an hour when you do not think He will.

Take, Eat, my Body and Drink my blood in remembrance of me—Matthew 26:26-28

While they were eating, Jesus took some bread, and after a blessing, He broke it and gave it to the disciples, and said, "Take, eat; this is My body." And when He had taken a cup and given thanks, He gave it to them, saying, "Drink from it, all of you; for this is My blood of the covenant, which is poured out for many for forgiveness of sins."

Watch and Pray—Matthew 26:41

Watch and pray so that you will not fall into temptation. The spirit is willing, but the flesh is weak.

Worship God alone—Luke 4:8

Jesus answered, "It is written: 'Worship the Lord your God and serve Him only."

I will make you fishers of men—Matthew 4:19

"Come, follow me," Jesus said, "and I will send you out to fish for people."

The Goal

Honour God's Law—Matthew 5:17-18

Do not think that I came to abolish the Law or the Prophets; I did not come to abolish but to fulfill. For truly I say to you, until heaven and earth pass away, not the smallest letter or stroke shall pass from the Law until all is accomplished. Whoever then annuls one of the least of these commandments, and teaches others to do the same, shall be called least in the kingdom of heaven; but whoever keeps and teaches them, he shall be called great in the kingdom of heaven.

Don't use vain repetitions when praying—Matthew 6:7-8.

And when you are praying, do not use meaningless repetition as the Gentiles do, for they suppose that they will be heard for their many words. So do not be like them; for your Father knows what you need before you ask Him.

Pray to God the Father—Matthew 6:8-13

Do not be like them, for your Father knows what you need before you ask Him. This, then, is how you should pray: "Our Father in heaven, hallowed be your Name, Your Kingdom come, Your will be done, on earth as it is in heaven. Give us today our daily bread. And forgive us our debts, as we also have forgiven our debtors. And lead us not into temptation, but deliver us from the evil one."

Keep asking, seeking and knocking—Luke 11:9-13

So I say to you, ask, and it will be given to you; seek, and you will find; knock, and it will be opened to you. For everyone who asks, receives; and he who seeks, finds; and to him who knocks, it will be opened. Now suppose one of you fathers is asked by his son for a fish; he will not give him a snake instead of a fish, will he? Or if he is asked for an egg, he will not give him a scorpion, will he? If you then, being evil, know how to give good gifts to your children, how much more will your heavenly Father give the Holy Spirit to those who ask Him?

Appendix B: Biblical References of What Jesus Wants...

Let the dead bury their dead—Matthew 8:22

But Jesus told him, "Follow me, and let the dead bury their own dead."

Ask the Lord of the harvest, therefore, to send out workers into his harvest field—Matthew 9:37-38

Then He said to His disciples, "The harvest is plentiful, but the workers are few. Therefore beseech the Lord of the harvest to send out workers into His harvest."

Repent of your sins—Luke 15:7-10

I tell you that in the same way, there will be more joy in heaven over one sinner who repents than over ninety-nine righteous persons who need no repentance. Or what woman, if she has ten silver coins and loses one coin, does not light a lamp and sweep the house and search carefully until she finds it? When she has found it, she calls together her friends and neighbours, saying, 'Rejoice with me, for I have found the coin which I had lost!' In the same way, I tell you, there is joy in the presence of the angels of God over one sinner who repents.

Have childlike faith—Luke 18:17

Truly I tell you, anyone who will not receive the kingdom of God like a little child will never enter it.

Believe in Jesus—John 14:6.

Jesus answered, "I am the way and the truth and the life. No one comes to the Father except through Me."

Don't be distracted from spending time with the Lord—Luke 10:38-42

Now as they were traveling along, He entered a village; and a woman named Martha welcomed Him into her home. She had a sister called Mary, who was seated at the Lord's feet, listening to His word. But Martha was distracted with all her preparations; and she came up to Him and said, "Lord, do You not care that my sister has left me to do all the serving alone? Then tell her to help me." But the Lord answered and said to her, "Martha, Martha, you are worried and bothered about so many things; but only one thing is necessary, for Mary has chosen the good part, which shall not be taken away from her."

Receive power—Luke 24:49

I am going to send you what my Father has promised; but stay in the city until you have been clothed with power from on high.

Keep My Commandments—John 14:15

If you love me, keep my commands.

3. Love your Neighbours

Love Your Neighbor—Matthew 22:39-40

The second is like it, 'YOU SHALL LOVE YOUR NEIGHBOR AS YOURSELF.' On these two commandments depend the whole Law and the Prophets.

Love, bless and pray for your enemies—Matthew 5:43-48

You have heard that it was said, 'YOU SHALL LOVE YOUR NEIGHBOR and hate your enemy.' But I say to you, love your enemies and pray for those who persecute you, so that you may be sons of your Father who is in heaven; for He causes His sun to rise on the evil and the good, and sends rain on the righteous and the unrighteous. For if you love those who love you, what reward do you have? Do not even the tax collectors do the same? If you greet only your brothers, what more are you doing than others? Do not even the Gentiles do the same? Therefore you are to be perfect, as your heavenly Father is perfect.

Forgive others—Matthew 6:12

And forgive us our debts, as we also have forgiven our debtors.

APPENDIX B: BIBLICAL REFERENCES OF WHAT JESUS WANTS...

Forgive Offenders—Matthew 18:21-22

Then Peter came and said to Him, "Lord, how often shall my brother sin against me and I forgive him? Up to seven times?" Jesus said to him, "I do not say to you, up to seven times, but up to seventy times seven."

Minister to others as you would to Jesus Himself— Matthew 25:34-46.

"Then the King will say to those on His right, 'Come, you who are blessed of My Father, inherit the kingdom prepared for you from the foundation of the world. For I was hungry, and you gave Me something to eat; I was thirsty, and you gave Me something to drink; I was a stranger, and you invited Me in; naked, and you clothed Me; I was sick, and you visited Me; I was in prison, and you came to Me.' Then the righteous will answer Him, 'Lord, when did we see You hungry, and feed You, or thirsty, and give You something to drink? And when did we see You a stranger, and invite You in, or naked, and clothe You? When did we see You sick, or in prison, and come to You?' The King will answer and say to them, 'Truly I say to you, to the extent that you did it to one of these brothers of Mine, even the least of them, you did it to Me.'"

Don't call your brother a fool—Matthew 5:22, 12:36

But I tell you that anyone who is angry with a brother or sister will be subject to judgment. Again, anyone who says to a brother or sister, 'Raca,' is answerable to the court. And anyone who says, 'You fool!' will be in danger of the fire of hell.

Go to Offenders and privately rebuke a brother— Matthew 18:15

If your brother or sister sins, go and point out their fault, just between the two of you. If they listen to you, you have won them over.

Quietly do good for God's praise alone—Matthew 6:1-4

Beware of practicing your righteousness before men to be noticed by them; otherwise you have no reward with your Father who is in heaven. So when you give to the poor, do not sound a trumpet before you, as the hypocrites do in the synagogues and in the streets, so that they may be honoured by men. Truly I say to you, they have their reward in full. But when you give to the poor, do not let your left hand know what your right hand is doing, so that your giving will be in secret; and your Father who sees what is done in secret will reward you.

Treat others as you like to be treated—Matthew 7:12

So in everything, do to others what you would have them do to you, for this sums up the Law and the Prophets.

Act with compassion and not prejudice towards others— Luke 10:30-37

Jesus replied and said, "A man was going down from Jerusalem to Jericho, and fell among robbers, and they stripped him and beat him, and went away leaving him half dead. And by chance a priest was going down on that road, and when he saw him, he passed by on the other side. Likewise a Levite also, when he came to the place and saw him, passed by on the other side. But a Samaritan, who was on a journey, came upon him; and when he saw him, he felt compassion, and came to him and bandaged up his wounds, pouring oil and wine on them; and he put him on his own beast, and brought him to an inn and took care of him. On the next day he took out two denarii and gave them to the innkeeper and said, 'Take care of him; and whatever more you spend, when I return I will repay you.' Which of these three do you think proved to be a neighbour to the man who fell into the robbers' hands?" And he said, "The one who showed mercy toward him." Then Jesus said to him, "Go and do the same."

Bring in the Poor. Invite the poor to eat with you— Luke 14:13-14

But when you give a reception, invite the poor, the crippled, the lame, the blind, and you will be blessed, since they do not have the means to repay you; for you will be repaid at the resurrection of the righteous.

Appendix B: Biblical References of What Jesus Wants...

Humble yourself and take the lowest position—Luke 14:8-11

When you are invited by someone to a wedding feast, do not take the place of honour, for someone more distinguished than you may have been invited by him, and he who invited you both will come and say to you, 'Give your place to this man,' and then in disgrace you proceed to occupy the last place. But when you are invited, go and recline at the last place, so that when the one who has invited you comes, he may say to you, 'Friend, move up higher'; then you will have honour in the sight of all who are at the table with you. For everyone who exalts himself will be humbled, and he who humbles himself will be exalted.

Be Reconciled—Matthew 5:23-24

Therefore if you are presenting your offering at the altar, and there remember that your brother has something against you, leave your offering there before the altar and go; first be reconciled to your brother, and then come and present your offering.

4. Family

Despise Not Little Ones—Matthew 18:10

See that you do not despise one of these little ones. For I tell you that their angels in heaven always see the face of my Father in heaven.

Do not look with lust at another this is adultery in the heart—Matthew 5:27-28

You have heard that it was said, 'YOU SHALL NOT COMMIT ADULTERY'; but I say to you that everyone who looks at a woman with lust for her has already committed adultery with her in his heart.

Honour Marriage—Matthew 19:6

So they are no longer two, but one flesh. Therefore what God has joined together, let no one separate.

Do not divorce and marry another, this is adultery— Matthew 5:32

But I tell you that anyone who divorces his wife, except for sexual immorality, makes her the victim of adultery, and anyone who marries a divorced woman commits adultery.

5. Abide in Me

Choose the Narrow Way—Matthew 7:13-14

Enter through the narrow gate; for the gate is wide and the way is broad that leads to destruction, and there are many who enter through it. For the gate is small and the way is narrow that leads to life, and there are few who find it.

Take up your cross—Matthew 16:24-26

And he who does not take his cross and follow after Me is not worthy of Me. He who has found his life will lose it, and he who has lost his life for My sake will find it.

Take My Yoke—Matthew 11:29

Take my yoke upon you and learn from me, for I am gentle and humble in heart, and you will find rest for your souls.

Follow Jesus—Matthew 4:19

"Come, follow me," Jesus said, "and I will send you out to fish for people."

Rejoice and be glad, when people insult you, persecute you and falsely say all kinds of evil against you because of me—Matthew 5:11-12

Blessed are you when people insult you and persecute you, and falsely say all kinds of evil against you because of Me. Rejoice and be glad, for your reward in heaven is great; for in the same way they persecuted the prophets who were before you.

Appendix B: Biblical References of What Jesus Wants...

Be perfect, therefore, as your heavenly Father is perfect—Matthew 5:46-48

For if you love those who love you, what reward do you have? Do not even the tax collectors do the same? If you greet only your brothers, what more are you doing than others? Do not even the Gentiles do the same? Therefore you are to be perfect, as your heavenly Father is perfect.

Don't be anxious—Matthew 6:25-34

For this reason I say to you, do not be worried about your life, as to what you will eat or what you will drink; nor for your body, as to what you will put on. Is not life more than food, and the body more than clothing? Look at the birds of the air, that they do not sow, nor reap nor gather into barns, and yet your heavenly Father feeds them. Are you not worth much more than they? And who of you by being worried can add a single hour to his life? And why are you worried about clothing? Observe how the lilies of the field grow; they do not toil nor do they spin, yet I say to you that not even Solomon in all his glory clothed himself like one of these. But if God so clothes the grass of the field, which is alive today and tomorrow is thrown into the furnace, will He not much more clothe you? You of little faith! Do not worry then, saying, 'What will we eat?' or 'What will we drink?' or 'What will we wear for clothing?' For the Gentiles eagerly seek all these things; for your heavenly Father knows that you need all these things. But seek first His kingdom and His righteousness, and all these things will be added to you. So do not worry about tomorrow; for tomorrow will care for itself. Each day has enough trouble of its own.

When you pray, fast or give do it secretly—Matthew 6:5-8

And when you pray, do not be like the hypocrites, for they love to pray standing in the synagogues and on the street corners to be seen by others. Truly I tell you, they have received their reward in full. But when you pray, go into your room, close the door and pray to your Father, who is unseen. Then your Father, who sees what is done in secret, will reward you. And when you pray, do not keep on babbling like pagans, for they think they will be heard because of their many words. Do not be like them, for your Father knows what you need before you ask him.

Rejoice when you are persecuted—Luke 6:22-23

Blessed are you when men hate you, and ostracize you, and insult you, and scorn your name as evil, for the sake of the Son of Man. Be glad in that day and leap for joy, for behold, your reward is great in heaven. For in the same way their fathers used to treat the prophets.

Deny Yourself—Luke 9:23

Then he said to them all: "Whoever wants to be my disciple must deny themselves and take up their cross daily and follow me."

Be Born Again—John 3:7

You should not be surprised at my saying, 'You must be born again.'

Live in Me and live in My love—John 15:4

As the Father has loved me, so have I loved you. Now remain in my love.

Beware of Covetousness—Luke 12:15

Then he said to them, "Watch out! Be on your guard against all kinds of greed; life does not consist in an abundance of possessions."

Don't swear an oath—Matthew 5:33-37

"Again, you have heard that the ancients were told, 'YOU SHALL NOT MAKE FALSE VOWS, BUT SHALL FULFILL YOUR VOWS TO THE LORD.' But I say to you, make no oath at all, either by heaven, for it is the throne of God, or by the earth, for it is the footstool of His feet, or by Jerusalem, for it is THE CITY OF THE GREAT KING. Nor shall you make an oath by your head, for you cannot make one hair white or black. But let your statement be, 'Yes, yes' or 'No, no'; anything beyond these is of evil."

Appendix B: Biblical References of What Jesus Wants...

Store your riches in heaven not on earth—Matthew 6:19-21

"Do not store up for yourselves treasures on earth, where moth and rust destroy, and where thieves break in and steal. But store up for yourselves treasures in heaven, where neither moth nor rust destroys, and where thieves do not break in or steal; for where your treasure is, there your heart will be also."

Resolve issues outside a court of law—Matthew 5:25

Make friends quickly with your opponent at law while you are with him on the way, so that your opponent may not hand you over to the judge, and the judge to the officer, and you be thrown into prison.

6. Honour Your Parents

Honour Your Parents—Matthew 15:4

"For God said, 'HONOR YOUR FATHER AND MOTHER.'"

7. Render unto Caesar

Render to Caesar. Pay your taxes and give to God what is his—Matthew 22:19-21

"Show Me the coin used for the poll-tax." And they brought Him a denarius. And He said to them, "Whose likeness and inscription is this?" They said to Him, "Caesar's." Then He said to them, "Then render to Caesar the things that are Caesar's; and to God the things that are God's."

8. Go the Extra Mile

Do more than expected, go the 2nd mile—Matthew 5:38-41

"You have heard that it was said, 'AN EYE FOR AN EYE, AND A TOOTH FOR A TOOTH.' But I say to you, do not resist an evil person; but whoever slaps you on your right cheek, turn the other to him also. If anyone wants to sue you and take your shirt, let him have your coat also. Whoever forces you to go one mile, go with him two."

9. Stewardship

Let your light shine before men—Matthew 5:16

Let your light shine before men in such a way that they may see your good works, and glorify your Father who is in heaven.

Be a Faithful Servant—Matthew 25:21

"His master replied, 'Well done, good and faithful servant! You have been faithful with a few things; I will put you in charge of many things. Come and share your master's happiness!'"

10. Leadership

Feed My Sheep—John 21:15-16

So when they had finished breakfast, Jesus said to Simon Peter, "Simon, son of John, do you love Me more than these?" He said to Him, "Yes, Lord; You know that I love You." He said to him, "Tend My lambs." He said to him again a second time, "Simon, son of John, do you love Me?" He said to Him, "Yes, Lord; You know that I love You." He said to him, "Shepherd My sheep."

Be Wise as Serpents—Matthew 10:16

I am sending you out like sheep among wolves. Therefore be as shrewd as snakes and as innocent as doves.

Be on your guard against the yeast of the Pharisees—Matthew 16:6

"Be careful," Jesus said to them. "Be on your guard against the yeast of the Pharisees and Sadducees."

Do Not Cast Pearls. Don't waste time on argumentative people—Matthew 7:6

Do not give what is holy to dogs, and do not throw your pearls before swine, or they will trample them under their feet, and turn and tear you to pieces.

APPENDIX B: BIBLICAL REFERENCES OF WHAT JESUS WANTS...

Don't sell things in God's house—Mark 11:15-17

He entered the temple and began to drive out those who were buying and selling in the temple, and overturned the tables of the money changers and the seats of those who were selling doves; and He would not permit anyone to carry merchandise through the temple. And He began to teach and say to them, "Is it not written, 'MY HOUSE SHALL BE CALLED A HOUSE OF PRAYER FOR ALL THE NATIONS'? But you have made it a ROBBERS' DEN."

Beware of False Prophets—Matthew 7:15

"Watch out for false prophets. They come to you in sheep's clothing, but inwardly they are ferocious wolves.

Be a Servant—Matthew 20:26-28

It is not this way among you, but whoever wishes to become great among you shall be your servant, and whoever wishes to be first among you shall be your slave; just as the Son of Man did not come to be served, but to serve, and to give His life a ransom for many.

11. Seek the Kingdom of God

Seek First God's Kingdom—Matthew 6:33

But seek first his kingdom and his righteousness, and all these things will be given to you as well.

Don't fear people—fear God—Matthew 10:28

Do not be afraid of those who kill the body but cannot kill the soul. Rather, be afraid of the One who can destroy both soul and body in hell.

Be baptized—Matthew 28:19

Therefore go and make disciples of all nations, baptizing them in the name of the Father and of the Son and of the Holy Spirit.

The Goal

Build on the rock of obedience to Jesus otherwise you will fall—Luke 6:47-49

"Everyone who comes to Me and hears My words and acts on them, I will show you whom he is like: he is like a man building a house, who dug deep and laid a foundation on the rock; and when a flood occurred, the torrent burst against that house and could not shake it, because it had been well built."

Don't call Jesus Lord when you don't obey Him—Luke 6:46

"Why do you call me, 'Lord, Lord,' and do not do what I say?"

APPENDIX C

The Kingdom of God

1. Who does it belong to? Who can enter the Kingdom?

Matthew 5:3   Blessed are the poor in spirit, for theirs is the kingdom of heaven.

Matthew 5:10   Blessed are those who are persecuted because of righteousness, for theirs is the kingdom of heaven.

Matthew 5:20   For I tell you that unless your righteousness surpasses that of the Pharisees and the teachers of the law, you will certainly not enter the kingdom of heaven.

Matthew 7:21   "Not everyone who says to me, 'Lord, Lord,' will enter the kingdom of heaven, but only he who does the will of my Father who is in heaven."

Matthew 18:3   And he said: "I tell you the truth, unless you change and become like little children, you will never enter the kingdom of heaven."

Matthew 18:4   Therefore, whoever humbles himself like this child is the greatest in the kingdom of heaven.

Matthew 19:14   Jesus said, "Let the little children come to me, and do not hinder them, for the kingdom of heaven belongs to such as these."

Matthew 21:43   "Therefore I tell you that the kingdom of God will be taken away from you and given to a people who will produce its fruit."

The Goal

Matthew 10:14	When Jesus saw this, he was indignant. He said to them, "Let the little children come to me, and do not hinder them, for the kingdom of God belongs to such as these."
Mark 10:15	I tell you the truth, anyone who will not receive the kingdom of God like a little child will never enter it.
Luke 6:20	Looking at his disciples, he said: "Blessed are you who are poor, for yours is the kingdom of God."
Luke 18:16	But Jesus called the children to him and said, "Let the little children come to me, and do not hinder them, for the kingdom of God belongs to such as these."
Luke 18:17	I tell you the truth, anyone who will not receive the kingdom of God like a little child will never enter it.
John 3:5	Jesus answered, "I tell you the truth, no one can enter the kingdom of God unless he is born of water and the Spirit."
Acts 14:22	Strengthening the disciples and encouraging them to remain true to the faith. "We must go through many hardships to enter the kingdom of God," they said.
Matthew 8:11	I say to you that many will come from the east and the west, and will take their places at the feast with Abraham, Isaac and Jacob in the kingdom of heaven.
Mark 10:24	The disciples were amazed at his words. But Jesus said again, "Children, how hard it is to enter the kingdom of God!"
Luke 13:29	People will come from east and west and north and south, and will take their places at the feast in the kingdom of God.
John 3:3	In reply Jesus declared, "I tell you the truth, no one can see the kingdom of God unless he is born again."

Appendix C: The Kingdom of God

2 Thessalonians 1:5   All this is evidence that God's judgment is right, and as a result you will be counted worthy of the kingdom of God, for which you are suffering.

2. Who does it not belong to?

Matthew 21:31   "Which of the two did what his father wanted?" "The first," they answered. Jesus said to them, "I tell you the truth, the tax collectors and the prostitutes are entering the kingdom of God ahead of you."

Matthew 19:23   Then Jesus said to his disciples, "I tell you the truth, it is hard for a rich man to enter the kingdom of heaven."

Matthew 23:13   "Woe to you, teachers of the law and Pharisees, you hypocrites! You shut the kingdom of heaven in men's faces. You yourselves do not enter, nor will you let those enter who are trying to."

Matthew 19:24   Again I tell you, it is easier for a camel to go through the eye of a needle than for a rich man to enter the kingdom of God.

Mark 10:23   Jesus looked around and said to his disciples, "How hard it is for the rich to enter the kingdom of God!"

Mark 10:25   It is easier for a camel to go through the eye of a needle than for a rich man to enter the kingdom of God.

Luke 13:28   "There will be weeping there, and gnashing of teeth, when you see Abraham, Isaac and Jacob and all the prophets in the kingdom of God, but you yourselves thrown out."

Luke 18:24   Jesus looked at him and said, "How hard it is for the rich to enter the kingdom of God!"

Luke 18:25   Indeed, it is easier for a camel to go through the eye of a needle than for a rich man to enter the kingdom of God.

1 Corinthians 6:9   Do you not know that the wicked will not inherit the kingdom of God? Do not be deceived: Neither the sexually immoral nor idolaters nor adulterers nor male prostitutes nor homosexual offenders.

1 Corinthians 6:10   Nor thieves nor the greedy nor drunkards nor slanderers nor swindlers will inherit the kingdom of God.

1 Corinthians 15:50   I declare to you, brothers, that flesh and blood cannot inherit the kingdom of God, nor does the perishable inherit the imperishable.

Galatians 5:21   And envy; drunkenness, orgies, and the like. I warn you, as I did before, that those who live like this will not inherit the kingdom of God.

3. Rank in the Kingdom

Matthew 11:11   I tell you the truth: Among those born of women there has not risen anyone greater than John the Baptist; yet he who is least in the kingdom of heaven is greater than he.

Matthew 18:1   At that time the disciples came to Jesus and asked, "Who is the greatest in the kingdom of heaven?"

Luke 7:28   I tell you, among those born of women there is no one greater than John; yet the one who is least in the kingdom of God is greater than he.

4. What is the Kingdom of God like?

Matthew 13:24   Jesus told them another parable: "The kingdom of heaven is like a man who sowed good seed in his field."

Matthew 13:31   He told them another parable: "The kingdom of heaven is like a mustard seed, which a man took and planted in his field."

Appendix C: The Kingdom of God

Matthew 13:33	He told them still another parable: "The kingdom of heaven is like yeast that a woman took and mixed into a large amount of flour until it worked all through the dough."
Matthew 13:44	The kingdom of heaven is like treasure hidden in a field. When a man found it, he hid it again, and then in his joy went and sold all he had and bought that field.
Matthew 13:45	Again, the kingdom of heaven is like a merchant looking for fine pearls.
Matthew 13:47	Once again, the kingdom of heaven is like a net that was let down into the lake and caught all kinds of fish.
Matthew 18:23	Therefore, the kingdom of heaven is like a king who wanted to settle accounts with his servants.
Matthew 20:1	For the kingdom of heaven is like a landowner who went out early in the morning to hire men to work in his vineyard.
Matthew 22:2	The kingdom of heaven is like a king who prepared a wedding banquet for his son.
Matthew 25:1	At that time the kingdom of heaven will be like ten virgins who took their lamps and went out to meet the bridegroom.
Mark 4:26	He also said, "This is what the kingdom of God is like. A man scatters seed on the ground."
Mark 4:30	Again he said, "What shall we say the kingdom of God is like, or what parable shall we use to describe it?"
Luke 13:18	Then Jesus asked, "What is the kingdom of God like? What shall I compare it to?"
Luke 13:20	Again he asked, "What shall I compare the kingdom of God to?"

The Goal

Romans 14:17	For the kingdom of God is not a matter of eating and drinking, but of righteousness, peace and joy in the Holy Spirit.
1 Corinthians 4:20	For the kingdom of God is not a matter of talk but of power.

5. Where is the kingdom?

Matthew 3:2	and saying, "Repent, for the kingdom of heaven is near."
Matthew 4:17	From that time on Jesus began to preach, "Repent, for the kingdom of heaven is near."
Matthew 10:7	As you go, preach this message: 'The kingdom of heaven is near.'
Matthew 12:28	But if I drive out demons by the Spirit of God, then the kingdom of God has come upon you.
Mark 1:15	"The time has come," he said. "The kingdom of God is near. Repent and believe the good news!"
Mark 12:34	When Jesus saw that he had answered wisely, he said to him, "You are not far from the kingdom of God." And from then on no one dared ask him any more questions.
Luke 10:9	Heal the sick who are there and tell them, 'The kingdom of God is near you.'
Luke 10:11	Even the dust of your town that sticks to our feet we wipe off against you. Yet be sure of this: The kingdom of God is near.
Luke 17:21	"Nor will people say, 'Here it is,' or 'There it is,' because the kingdom of God is within you."
Luke 19:11	While they were listening to this, he went on to tell them a parable, because he was near Jerusalem and the people thought that the kingdom of God was going to appear at once.
Luke 21:31	Even so, when you see these things happening, you know that the kingdom of God is near.

Appendix C: The Kingdom of God

Luke 22:16   For I tell you, I will not eat it again until it finds fulfillment in the kingdom of God.

Luke 22:18   For I tell you I will not drink again of the fruit of the vine until the kingdom of God comes.

6. Who is least in the Kingdom of Heaven?

Matthew 5:19   Anyone who breaks one of the least of these commandments and teaches others to do the same will be called least in the kingdom of heaven, but whoever practices and teaches these commands will be called great in the kingdom of heaven.

7. Who advances (the work of) the kingdom?

Matthew 11:12   From the days of John the Baptist until now, the kingdom of heaven has been forcefully advancing, and forceful men lay hold of it.

Luke 8:1   After this, Jesus traveled about from one town and village to another, proclaiming the good news of the kingdom of God. The Twelve were with him.

Luke 9:2   and he sent them out to preach the kingdom of God and to heal the sick.

Luke 9:11   but the crowds learned about it and followed him. He welcomed them and spoke to them about the kingdom of God, and healed those who needed healing.

Luke 9:60   Jesus said to him, "Let the dead bury their own dead, but you go and proclaim the kingdom of God."

Luke 9:62   Jesus replied, "No one who puts his hand to the plow and looks back is fit for service in the kingdom of God."

Luke 11:20   But if I drive out demons by the finger of God, then the kingdom of God has come to you.

The Goal

Luke 14:15   When one of those at the table with him heard this, he said to Jesus, "Blessed is the man who will eat at the feast in the kingdom of God."

Luke 16:16   The Law and the Prophets were proclaimed until John. Since that time, the good news of the kingdom of God is being preached, and everyone is forcing his way into it.

Luke 18:29   "I tell you the truth," Jesus said to them, "no one who has left home or wife or brothers or parents or children for the sake of the kingdom of God."

Acts 1:3   After his suffering, he showed himself to these men and gave many convincing proofs that he was alive. He appeared to them over a period of forty days and spoke about the kingdom of God.

Acts 8:12   But when they believed Philip as he preached the good news of the kingdom of God and the name of Jesus Christ, they were baptized, both men and women.

Acts 19:8   Paul entered the synagogue and spoke boldly there for three months, arguing persuasively about the kingdom of God.

Acts 28:23   They arranged to meet Paul on a certain day, and came in even larger numbers to the place where he was staying. From morning till evening he explained and declared to them the kingdom of God and tried to convince them about Jesus from the Law of Moses and from the Prophets.

Acts 28:31   Boldly and without hindrance he preached the kingdom of God and taught about the Lord Jesus Christ.

8. *Secrets of the Kingdom*

Matthew 13:11   He replied, "The knowledge of the secrets of the kingdom of heaven has been given to you, but not to them."

Appendix C: The Kingdom of God

Matthew 13:52   He said to them, "Therefore every teacher of the law who has been instructed about the kingdom of heaven is like the owner of a house who brings out of his storeroom new treasures as well as old."

Mark 4:11   He told them, "The secret of the kingdom of God has been given to you. But to those on the outside everything is said in parables."

Luke 8:10   He said, "The knowledge of the secrets of the kingdom of God has been given to you, but to others I speak in parables, so that, 'though seeing, they may not see; though hearing, they may not understand.'"

Luke 17:20   Once, having been asked by the Pharisees when the kingdom of God would come, Jesus replied, "The kingdom of God does not come with your careful observation."

9. Keys of the Kingdom

Matthew 16:19   I will give you the keys of the kingdom of heaven; whatever you bind on earth will be bound in heaven, and whatever you loose on earth will be loosed in heaven.

10. Other scriptures

Mark 14:25   "I tell you the truth, I will not drink again of the fruit of the vine until that day when I drink it anew in the kingdom of God."

Mark 15:43   Joseph of Arimathea, a prominent member of the Council, who was himself waiting for the kingdom of God, went boldly to Pilate and asked for Jesus' body.

Luke 4:43   But he said, "I must preach the good news of the kingdom of God to the other towns also, because that is why I was sent."

The Goal

Luke 9:27   I tell you the truth, some who are standing here will not taste death before they see the kingdom of God.

Luke 23:51   Who had not consented to their decision and action. He came from the Judean town of Arimathea and he was waiting for the kingdom of God.

Colossians 4:11   Jesus, who is called Justus, also sends greetings. These are the only Jews among my fellow workers for the kingdom of God, and they have proved a comfort to me.

Mark 9:1   And he said to them, "I tell you the truth, some who are standing here will not taste death before they see the kingdom of God come with power."

Mark 9:47   And if your eye causes you to sin, pluck it out. It is better for you to enter the kingdom of God with one eye than to have two eyes and be thrown into hell.

Matthew 19:12   For some are eunuchs because they were born that way; others were made that way by men; and others have renounced marriage because of the kingdom of heaven. The one who can accept this should accept it.

APPENDIX D

How to Hear the Voice of God

Hearing from God is easy. Since you are reading this section, you may not quite believe that. To begin, we need to embrace one simple truth: God wants to speak to you.

Some are afraid to look for a spiritual answer from God—afraid that they are not worthy, afraid of what He might say, afraid He will punish them. The truth is God is big. Jesus said, *"If [your child] asks for a fish, will [you] give him a snake? If you, then, though you are evil, know how to give good gifts to your children, how much more will your Father in heaven give good gifts to those who ask him!"*[28] He is inviting us to ask Him. Others are afraid they will be deceived. I encourage you to have more faith that God can speak to you than the devil has power to deceive you. We must believe that God will speak to us.

The process of hearing from God is described in the Bible. King David, the prophets, Jesus, and the apostles all heard from God very clearly and lived in a state of constant communication with their Heavenly Father. The setting for hearing God did differ from person to person. Jesus would draw away from the crowd where He could be alone. King David used to go to the temple and sit before the Lord. Elisha called for a minstrel to play so he could hear from God. Although in different settings, they all used the same four steps to hear from God. These steps were as follows:

1. They recognized that God speaks to them in their minds, in their thoughts.

2. They chose to hear, to listen, to see, and would draw away and become quiet.

3. They would focus the eyes of their hearts on the Lord, look for vision and listen to His flow of thoughts.

4. They would write down what they saw or heard so it could be shared with others.

God speaks to us in our thoughts. These thoughts may be words or images; but this is not the only way God speaks to us. Just as we have five physical senses, we have five spiritual senses, and God can speak to us using any of those senses. For the sake of learning how to hear God, we will start with the basics and look at the Biblical accounts of how King David and the prophet Habakkuk heard from God.

King David provides us with an excellent example of how he heard from God. He asked God about building His temple, and God gave Him very specific directions. Let's look at how he heard God.

King David rose to his feet and said:

"Listen to me, my brothers and my people. I had it in my heart to build a house as a place of rest for the ark of the covenant of the LORD"...Then David gave his son Solomon the plans for the portico of the temple, its buildings, its storerooms, its upper parts, its inner rooms and the place of atonement. He gave him the plans of all that the Spirit had put in his mind for the courts of the temple of the LORD and all the surrounding rooms, for the treasuries of the temple of God and for the treasuries for the dedicated things. He gave him instructions for the divisions of the priests and Levites, and for all the work of serving in the temple of the LORD, as well as for all the articles to be used in its service. He designated the weight of gold for all the gold articles to be used in various kinds of service, and the weight of silver for all the silver articles to be used in various kinds of service. He also gave him the plan for the chariot, that is, the cherubim of gold that spread their wings and shelter the ark of the covenant of the LORD. "All this," David said, "I have in writing from the hand of the LORD upon me, and he gave me understanding in all the details of the plan."29

Appendix D: How to Hear the Voice of God

We can see the four steps that David followed to hear God.

1. David knew God spoke to him in his mind.

2. David decided to inquire of the Lord about building the temple and quieted his heart before Him.

3. David tuned into the flow of God's voice, and the Lord began to speak to him. The Lord put the thoughts in David's mind. He told David how the temple should be built. He described how it should be organized, what it should look like, and how much gold and silver should be used for each item in the temple.

4. David wrote down what the Lord showed him, and he gave it to his son Solomon to build.

As I read David's account of this experience, I am amazed at the level of detail in the revelation the Lord gave him. The plans were precise and all encompassing. The process was not complex. King David simply asked God and heard God in his mind tell him what he was to do, and he wrote it down.

I wanted to learn how to do that, to hear God's plans for me. I went to a man who prophesied in a church. When I asked him how he knew God was speaking to him, he told me that he "just knew in his knower." I thought, you're a big help. I never did figure out how to hear God from him. Yet King David's approach was so simple. He just shared his heart with God, and God gave him specific thoughts in his mind. What could be easier? I could do that.

The prophet Habakkuk also heard from God the way King David did. Habakkuk recorded his experience. He said:

> "I will stand at my watch and station myself on the ramparts; I will look to see what He will say to me, and what answer I am to give to this complaint. Then the LORD replied: 'Write down the revelation and make it plain on tablets so that a herald may run with it.'"30

Again I could see the four steps.

1. Habakkuk knew God spoke to him in his mind.

The Goal

2. Habakkuk chose to hear from God and drew himself away to a place of solitude. He would go up the defensive wall (his watch) around his town to listen to God. This is such an important first step. We have to be quiet to hear God. He doesn't yell at us. He speaks to us in a quiet voice in our mind.

3. Habakkuk looked to see what God was saying. God speaks to us in both words and pictures; He will often give us images because it is faster. The saying "a picture is worth a thousand words" is so true. Habakkuk tuned into a flow of thoughts and images (the revelation) that were in his mind.

4. Habakkuk wrote them down.

I have found that God is not in a hurry and that He will speak slowly enough for me to write down what He is saying. Sometimes He only gives me one word at a time so I can write it down while He is speaking.

Jesus said we must become as little children to enter His kingdom. Little children are quite different from older children. Little children believe what their father says, they believe that their father knows everything, and they believe he can do everything. Little children find it easy to use their imagination when Mom or Dad read stories to them. For us to enter the kingdom of God and consistently hear from God, we have to step back and retrieve these beliefs and abilities in our lives.

Some believe that any use of their imagination to focus the eyes of their heart on the Lord is wrong, possibly new age or even idolatry. In the Hebrew language, the word *meditate* includes the meaning to imagine. We need to discard the false belief that we cannot use our imagination when we meditate on the Lord. We need to acknowledge that everything God made is good and God can use that part of our mind to communicate with us.

Some believe that God doesn't talk directly to people anymore. They believe that this type of communication passed away with the apostles. This is not true, God has not changed. He loves to communicate with us His children, and we need to break agreement with this false belief as well.

Appendix D: How to Hear the Voice of God

Personal Action

The truth is, God wants to talk to you and He has made it easy to do it. Let's start by learning how to listen for the voice of God.

Most of us have experienced having a song on our heart, and we find ourselves singing or humming along with the song. Try singing the song "Happy Birthday" in your mind.

When you can do this, check this box. ☐

Happy Birthday to You
Happy Birthday to You
Happy Birthday, Happy Birthday
Happy Birthday to You

Keep doing this until you are able to do it easily. This is the place in our mind where God speaks to us. God speaks to us as a stream of thoughts.

It is often said that children have a vivid imagination. When you were a child, did you imagine the story your mom or dad read to you? I remember my mother reading me the novel *Mysterious Island* by Jules Verne. Each lunch hour when I came home from school, she would read a chapter to me. I loved it. I could envision Captain Nemo and the Nautilus and the giant creatures that were in the story.

God also uses visions when he speaks to us. Visions are simply images that He gives us. He often uses images because a lot of information can be conveyed with a simple picture. To start seeing visions, you have to know where to look. In your mind, there is an imagination screen. We use this screen when we imagine images and scenes. We use our mind to create the images. When God gives us a vision, He uses this same screen. The difference is that He is the one who paints the picture and our mind is not involved.

Let's do an exercise to practice using your imagination screen. I want you to imagine your home. Check off the box when you can see each scene

1. Imagine the home you live in. ☐
2. Walk through the front door. ☐
3. Go into the kitchen. ☐
4. Open the fridge. ☐

The Goal

5. Find the apples. ☐
6. Choose a green one. ☐
7. Bite into the apple. ☐

You have just used your imagination screen. This ability was given to us by God so we can bring new ideas into being. At first you may find it difficult to imagine in colour, but keep at it and it will get easier.

Now that we know where to look and listen, let's try hearing from God. To start, we will focus the eyes of our hearts on the author of our faith, Jesus. We do this by simply imagining a Bible story. Children love to imagine a story. I would like you to become like a little child and just imagine this paraphrased story of Jesus and His disciples (John 21).

Jesus looked over the Sea of Galilee. He stood up on a grassy hill where the onshore breeze blew over the grass and caught His white robe and hair. He wanted to meet His disciples, who had gone out fishing that morning. Jesus knew that they had had a rough couple of days, so He planned to prepare breakfast for them. He had some fish and bread and walked down along the beach. You could hear the waves lapping against the shore. He built a small fire, cooked the fish, and was warming himself while he waited for His disciples to return.

As the disciples drew close to the shore, they could see a man on the beach but they did not recognize who He was. Jesus called to them and said, "Did you catch any fish?" They replied, "No we did not."

He called to them and said, "Let down your nets on the other side of your boat." The disciples did just as they were told and a large number of fish jumped into the net. The water was alive with fish. The sun reflected off their scales, and the water was shaking violently as the fish fought to get into the net. Nathaniel looked at Peter with astonishment. The disciples had caught so many fish they could not pull the net into the boat.

Peter looked from the fish to the man on the beach. John said, "It is the Lord." Peter wrapped himself in his robe, jumped into the water, and swam towards the beach. Peter ran up to Jesus and fell on his face at His feet. Jesus saw him and began to speak to him. After a few moments, Peter went to help the other disciples bring in the net of fish and Jesus went back and sat by the fire.

Appendix D: How to Hear the Voice of God

- Now go and sit down beside Jesus at the fire and look at him right in the face. Spend some time looking at Him. After a few moments of looking at Him, ask Him this question, "Do you love me?"

- Write down what Jesus says or does.

You have just heard from the Lord. I gave you a question to which there is only one answer, "Yes," because I want you to experience how the Lord says yes to you. In most cases it is very personal.

The story you imagined was used to focus your eyes on the Lord and on the written word of God. It was used to help you to make the transition from the written word of God to the spoken word of God. Let's do some more hearing and seeing.

- Now go back to the scene of Jesus sitting at the fire and look at Him again. Ask Him, "Please tell me more."

- Write down what Jesus says or does.

You have just heard from God. You have followed the four steps.

1. You recognized God speaks to you in your mind.

2. You quieted your heart by imagining the Bible story.

3. You focused the eyes and ears of your heart on the Lord and you tuned into the flow of thoughts that come from God.

4. You wrote it down.

Jesus wants to meet with you face to face. He is not restricted by time or space. He will meet with you in your mind since according to King David, this is the realm of spiritual connection.

Let's do one final exercise. Please go back to where you saw Jesus by the fire and look at Him again.

- Ask Him this question: "What would You like to say to me today?"

- Write down what Jesus says or does.

- Call a friend and tell them you are practicing hearing from God. Describe what you heard Jesus say or do and ask them if it sounds like God to them.

The Goal

After we have written down what God says, we can test it to ensure that it is God's word. There are several tests we can do.

1. First, we test it against the Bible. God will not contradict His written word.

2. Second, we test it against the characteristics of our Heavenly Father: God is love, God is kind, God is merciful. God will not say things that are harsh, mean-spirited, or cynical. All true prophetic words build up, encourage, and comfort. (I Corinthians 14:3)

3. Third, we test it against the names of God. God will not contradict His own names. Here are some of the names of God:
   - Jehovah Elohim—The Lord Is God
   - Jehovah Nissi—The Lord Is My Banner
   - Jehovah Rophi—The Lord Who Heals Me
   - Jehovah Jireh—The Lord Who Provides
   - Jehovah Tzadekenu—The Lord Our Righteousness
   - Jehovah Shalom—The Lord of Peace
   - Jehovah Rohi—The Lord Is My Shepherd
   - Jehovah Shammah—The Lord Is Here

4. We test it with others. The body of Christ will witness to true words. There is great safety when you are accountable to someone else who will give you their honest opinion.

Now that you have heard God's voice I invite you to return to the book and continue your journey with Him. Take this opportunity to talk with Him and hear His will for your life.

APPENDIX E

How to Be Closer to God

You may be wanting to improve your relationship with God. Or, you may want to be sure that you will go to heaven when you die. You may have enjoyed the journaling which you have read in this book, and long to be able to have the same kind of experience in your own life. The wonderful thing is, you can! Here's how...

The Bible teaches that God hungers to share His love with you. In the Garden of Eden, God walked and talked with Adam and Eve in the cool of the day. That is what God wants to do with each of us, also. He yearns to be able to share His love with us and have us share our hearts with Him on a daily basis. As our Creator and Sustainer, He knows what we need even more than we do, and He answers our questions even before we ask.

God's heart was broken when sin entered into Adam and Eve's lives and stole away that relationship He had with them. The tempter tempted Adam and Eve to live like gods themselves, rather than enjoy the flow of God's life through them. In choosing to look to self, rather than looking beyond to the wonderful Giver of Life, Adam and Eve cut off much of the flow of God within them.

So God sent His Son, Jesus of Nazareth, in the form of a man, to remove the sin which separated mankind's heart from the heart of God. By entering the world as a man, God was able to take the sins of the entire world upon His own shoulders and pay the penalty of this separation by allowing His Son, Jesus Christ, to be separated from Him for a moment of time. That is why Jesus cried out while dying on the cross, *"My God, My God, why have You forsaken Me?"* However, in forsaking

The Goal

His Son for a moment of time, God was restoring the opportunity for you and me to return to the experience of the Garden of Eden and, once again, have fellowship with Almighty God. Once again, we could walk with Him in the cool of the day and share our lives with Him and have God share His life with us.

So our relationship with God can be enhanced. We can be sure of going to heaven by receiving the sacrifice of Jesus' life for our sins. The steps are quite clearly laid out in the Bible.

The steps to salvation are as follows:

1. I repent (change my mind) for being master of my own life and living separate from God.

2. I accept Christ's death on the cross which purchases my rescue from the devil's dominion.

3. I receive You, Jesus, as MY personal Lord, King, Commander and Saviour.

4. I welcome You, Holy Spirit, into my life to rescue and empower me, and to restore me to intimacy with my Heavenly Father.

A Prayer of Response

If you want a closer relationship with God, if you want to know for certain that when you die you will go to heaven, then offer the following prayer to God, from the depths of your heart. Pray aloud, slowly, meaningfully, staying open to experiencing the flow of your heart, including flowing pictures, words and emotions.

> *Precious Holy Spirit, do a work in my heart as I offer the following prayer to God.*
>
> *God, I come to You in the name of Your Son, the Lord Jesus Christ. I acknowledge that I have sinned and fallen short of Your ways. I repent (change my mind) for being master of my own life and living separate from God. I accept Christ's death on the cross which purchases my rescue from the devil's dominion. I receive You, Jesus, as MY personal Lord, King, Commander and Saviour. I welcome You, Holy Spirit, into my life to rescue and empower me, and to restore me to intimacy with my Heavenly Father.*

Appendix E: How to Be Closer to God

I confess with my mouth that Jesus Christ is the Son of God and the Lord of my life. I invite You, Jesus, to have first place in my heart and my life.

I believe God raised Jesus from the dead, and that He is alive in my heart today. I forsake any evil ways and thoughts which I have harbored, and this day turn my life over to Jesus. I ask, Jesus, that You fill my heart and my mind with Your ways and Your thoughts and that You begin a transforming work from within my heart and my spirit.

By believing in Jesus and His life within me, I am assured a place in heaven with God. I receive eternal life this day. Thank You, Lord Jesus Christ. I yield myself right now to the moving of the Holy Spirit within my spirit. Holy Spirit, please make this very real in my heart and let me sense Your moving within me. May You seal this prayer this day.

Now just wait quietly for a few minutes in the presence of God and His Holy Spirit and see what you sense within. Lift up your eyes to Jesus and humbly receive His life within your soul.

Record in your journal today's date along with any impressions or sensations which you received in your heart and soul as you prayed this prayer.

Taking Your First Steps as a Christian

If you have just prayed the above prayer, I invite you to obtain a copy of the Bible and begin reading, starting with Matthew. I recommend you download the free Bible software e-Sword (www.e-sword.net). It has free training videos and a good number of translations to get you started in meditating on the Bible. Also I recommend the book *Basics in 21 Days* (www.cwgministries.org/store/basics-21-days) which begins teaching you how to live naturally supernaturally in the very first weeks of your Christian journey.

For additional information on how to hear God's voice or to learn how to be counselled by God, please contact Communion with God Ministries www.cwgministries.org

CWG Fulfillment Center, 3792 Broadway St., Buffalo, NY 14227
Email: mark@cluonline.com
Phone: 1-800-466-6961 or 716-681-4896
Fax: 716-685-3908

AUTHOR'S BIOGRAPHY

William and Susan Dupley

Bill and Sue have been ministering for over 30 years, preaching and leading worship on five continents. Together they minister renewal and teach adults and children how to hear the voice of God. Bill and Sue believe that the supernatural should be the natural for all believers and that every believer can impact their world for the kingdom of God as they hear God's will and follow His leading.

Bill and Sue's home church is Catch the Fire Toronto where they lead worship and have been ministering the "Toronto Blessing" to God's family. Together they have co-authored "Kids in Renewal," a dynamic Sunday school program that teaches children their Heavenly Father's heart for them, how to hear His voice, and how to receive and impart spiritual gifts.

Bill has also authored *The Secret Place*. This book is a personal story of how God's speaks to us and what He sounds like. It is designed so that you can develop your own Secret Place with your Heavenly Father. It is now available in five languages and distributed globally.

Bill and Sue are certified facilitators for Communion with God Ministries and have conducted seminars at Catch the Fire, Mission Fest, Releasers of Life, Iris Ministries, and many other churches in North America, Africa, Australia, Europe, and Asia. Their passion is for God's family to know their Heavenly Father and to hear His voice, so that they may live in the fullness of the gifts and the freedom that Jesus bought for them.

Bill and Sue came to the Lord in 1976. Since that time, the Lord has guided them through business careers, and they have experienced the blessing of the Lord in their business and ministry.

The Goal

Bill is currently a chief technologist in a global technology company, and Susan is a nurse. Susan is a graduate of the University of Toronto in Nursing Science, and Bill is a graduate of Ryerson University in Electronics Technology. Bill and Sue are affiliated with Catch the Fire and Communion with God Ministries.

Endnotes

1 Dupley, William. *The Secret Place*. ISBN 978-1-936860-01-2
2 John 5:19
3 Hebrews 12:1
4 Philippians 3:14
5 Matthew 5:14
6 Matthew 28:16-20. In Matthew 28:20 "I commanded," The root of this word is entellomai Strongs 1781,
http://biblehub.com/greek/1781.htm
Word Origin: from en and tellomai (to accomplish)
John 15:10 "commands," Greek word entolé Strong 1785
http://biblehub.com/greek/1785.htm
Root of entolé entellomai Strong 1781
7 John 15:10
8 Matthew 5:14-16
9 Genesis 41:1
10 http://www.hope-of-israel.org/josepheg.htm
11 http://www.cwgministries.org/blogs/why-do-good-companies-fail
12 Matthew 5:28
13 Hebrews 13:4.
14 Matthew 6:19
15 "Don't Laugh at Me" by Mark Willis
16 Luke 10:27
17 Luke 6:45
18 Psalm 100:2
19 Hebrews 12:2 NASB

20 Roman 12:2
21 Philippians 4:8
22 Luke 10:27
23 Mark 12:30-31
24 Mark 9:35
25 Mark 10;43-45
26 Matthew 5:38-40
27 Matthew 5:44 KJV
28 1 John 3:15.
29 Matthew 12:34
30 Ephesians 6:4
31 http://biblehub.com/greek/nouthesia_3559.htm
32 Mark 9:35
33 Matthew 11:29
34 Ephesians 5:24
35 http://en.wikipedia.org/wiki/Greek_words_for_love
36 Ephesians 5:25
37 Ephesians 5:21-24
38 http://biblehub.com/text/ephesians/5-22.htm
39 http://biblehub.com/text/ephesians/5-24.htm
40 http://biblehub.com/greek/5293.htm
41 John 15:1
42 John 15:4
43 Strong's Concordance 3306. menó
44 Galatians 5:22-23
45 Exodus 35:31-33
46 John 17:22
47 Ephesians 6:2-3
48 Ephesians 6:3
49 Mark 12:17
50 Mark 12:17
51 Roman 13:1
52 Ephesians 6:12
53 1 Timothy 2:1-2
54 Matthew 5:41
55 Luke 6:27-28
56 Matthew 25:21

Endnotes

57 http://biblehub.com/greek/2041.htm
58 Matthew 17:24-27
59 1 Timothy 5:18
60 2 Corinthians 9:7
61 Romans 12:1
62 2 Timothy 1:7
63 Colossians 3:15
64 Luke 10:29-37
65 Mark 7:9-13
66 1 Timothy 5:8
67 Luke 14:28
68 Mark 10:42-45
69 http://www.the7mountains.com/
70 Mark 10:42-45
71 Gillet, J., Cartwright, E., and Van Vugt, M. (2010). Selfish or servant leadership: Testing evolutionary predictions about leadership in coordination games. Personality and Individual Differences. doi:10.1016/j.paid.2010.06.003
http://en.wikipedia.org/wiki/Servant_leadership#cite_note-7
72 Matthew 11:28-30
73 Nehemiah 1:11
74 Matthew 6:33
75 Matthew 3:2
76 Luke 17:21
77 Matthew 12:28
78 Matthew 12:24
79 Romans 10:17
80 Revelation 12:11
81 1 Corinthians 2:4
82 John 14:12
83 Luke 8:1-2
84 2 Timothy 2:15
85 2 Timothy 3:16-17
86 Acts 17:11
87 John 5:19
88 James 2:14-17
89 Matthew 28:16-20

The Goal

[90] http://en.wikipedia.org/wiki/Disciple_%28Christianity%29
[91] Matthew 22:36-40
[92] John 15:9-10
[93] Luke 18:11

www.ingramcontent.com/pod-product-compliance
Ingram Content Group UK Ltd.
Pitfield, Milton Keynes, MK11 3LW, UK
UKHW022226230426
12048UKWH00016BA/1094